Purry Companion's

Happy, Meowy Christmas Devotional

Deborah A. Goshorn-Stenger

Our mission is to share the love of Jesus through His Word, nature, and creativity. We believe that God's beauty is all around us, if we'll pause to see it, and give Him honor and praise.

2 Pause and Praise Creations

Purry Companion's
Happy, Meowy Christmas Devotional

Copyright 2022 © by 2 Pause and Praise Creations

Requests for information should be directed to:
2 Pause and Praise Creations
5315 Long Street, Suite 518
McFarland, WI 53558

ISBN: 978-1-954690-16-5

Deborah Goshorn-Stenger, her husband, Douglas
Jeepers (L) and Muffin (R)

With Dedication

Dear Jesus,
This is our offering of love, gratitude, and praise.
May every line be like a song unto Your throne.

Dear Douglas,
I offer you a heartfelt "thank you" for being my right-hand—to hold as we walk, daily—to pray with, work with, to live and love with, in every step of this project. You're my best friend, and my earthly and heavenly treasure! I love you and cherish every day of our journey.

Dear Family and Friends, to those who "*believed*" in me, and the talent given by God's Spirit—to bring His creations to life —I appreciate your support and notes of encouragement.

A very special thank you, to my early readers/reviewers. I treasure your kindness and insights for this endeavor!

In loving memory of Doug's Dad, my father-in-love, Bob Stenger. You passed on your love for cats from your childhood to Doug, and he, to our home. This has been a precious gift to us. Their sweet companionship has been a reminder of your love, and our heavenly Father's devotion and care throughout our marriage.

Also in loving memory of my mom, Pauline Rubeck Goshorn, thank you for leaving a "paw print" of faith and courage, and for sharing my writing as part of your testimony. Your affection and purr-of-praise (humming) are missed by many!!

I am grateful to each of you, and my readers, and pray that this Prelude to the *Purry Companion's Series*, will bring you blessing, joy, and God's grace, nearly and dearly, to your hearts.

In His Love,

deborah goshorn-stenger

From the time I was a child, I remember loving Christmas. I adored the smells emanating throughout the house, baking by mom's side, and the family traditions like listening to my momma' read the Christmas story from Luke 2 each year. I loved our outing of cutting a fresh tree for the basement, and helping to decorate the fancy one that adorned the living room.

Christmas growing up was a festive time of carols playing and being sung. It held nights of going out and viewing lights. It meant the fireplace would be lit and set to sparkle with a special powder that made it come alive with iridescent colors. And it meant that cards got mailed, gifts got hidden (when we were young) and wrapped and given as we got older. And while our family was not wealthy, we always had a turkey with the trimmings, a number of gifts for each of us 'neath the tree, and the feeling of love to surround us.

In our own home, Doug and I have continued some of these same traditions. And when we added our first cat (Muffin, pictured on the right and our second one, Jeepers, on the left), it was like they too shared in the spirit of all that was wonderful, festive and precious about the yuletide season.

I hope the following entries, poems, prayers, meditations and excerpts from Scripture, bring you sweet remembrances or a fresh adoration and wonder, of the One we celebrate—Jesus.

What is bright-eyed and bushy-tailed?
What runs, jumps, and leaps,
To then be found, curled-up,
In a ball, fast asleep?
What uses its whiskers,
To guide its way?
What has a "hum" within it,
Like praise, everyday?
What can display affection,
Yet communicate a "hiss?"
What can draw us into companionship,
With a furry embrace and a delicate "kiss?"
What has spunk and spirit,
And moves with lithe and grace?
What creation of the Creator,
Teaches us, to look upon His face?
If by now you're thinking,
The feline, the cat ...
Then my glowing description,
Is on target—at that!
But I guess you can imagine,
That we were a bit surprised,
When we found Tiger Lily climbing ...
Then sleeping in the tree limbs,
Right before our very eyes.

This is to share Christmas with a cat! Perhaps giving us felines, is one way in which Jesus shows us His love and affectionate nature.

Feline Headliners
The "Maine" Character

Tiger Lily, our Maine Coon Mix
aka T.L. and Tilly

Supporting Actress   Supporting Actor

Jeeper-Joy
Our Black and white Long
haired domestic

Muffin-Willow
Our first cat
Short-haired, gray Tabby

See the Appendix for information about each of our purry companions.

How to use this Devotional

This work has been designed to have a creative, free-flowing narrative. It is intended for you to read as you wish. What do I mean? Read one entry a day or several at a time.

Read and absorb, at your own pace. But please, allow time to meditate—upon each picture, entry, Scripture, and feline-inspired concept. Use this as an enhancement of your personal time with God —when you have time—to delve into its insights and truths.

As to its parts? You'll notice some entries are poems, some are more prose in styles. Along the way, you'll find "Leaving a Paw Print," which provide Scripture references for you to use as a Bible study, and "A Purr of Prayer," which is just that! You'll also find prayers that are specific to the Biblical account, which will help you ponder the significance of Jesus' birth.

You will find a verse listing which will allow you to journal and commune with God. This devotional is perfect for your personal study and reflection, and would also be appropriate for small-group fellowship.

As you read page by page, I hope you will feel the Creator drawing you into a closer companionship. For He longs to be your Best Friend, Protector, and Guide.

The Account of Jesus' Birth

"And it came to pass in those days, that there went out a decree from Caesar Augustus that all the world should be taxed. (And this taxing was first made when Cyrenius was governor of Syria.) And all went to be taxed, every one into his own city. And Joseph also went up from Galilee, out of the city of Nazareth, into Judaea, unto the city of David, which is called Bethlehem; (because he was of the house and lineage of David:) To be taxed with Mary his espoused wife, being great with child.

And so it was, that, while they were there, the days were accomplished that she should be delivered. And she brought forth her firstborn son, and wrapped him in swaddling clothes, and laid him in a manger; because there was no room for them in the inn.

And there were in the same country shepherds abiding in the field, keeping watch over their flock by night. And, lo, the angel of the Lord came upon them, and the glory of the Lord shone round about them: and they were sore afraid. And the angel said unto them, Fear not: for, behold, I bring you good tidings of great joy, which shall be to all people. For unto you is born this day in the city of David a Saviour, which is Christ the Lord.

And this shall be a sign unto you; Ye shall find the babe wrapped in swaddling clothes, lying in a manger. And suddenly there was with the angel a multitude of the heavenly host praising God, and saying …

Glory to God in the highest, and on earth peace, good will toward men.

And it came to pass, as the angels were gone away from them into heaven, the shepherds said one to another, Let us now go even unto Bethlehem, and see this thing which is come to pass, which the Lord hath made known unto us.

And they came with haste, and found Mary, and Joseph, and the babe lying in a manger. And when they had seen it, they made known abroad the saying which was told them concerning this child. And all they that heard it wondered at those things which were told them by the shepherds. But Mary kept all these things, and pondered them in her heart. And the shepherds returned, glorifying and praising God for all the things that they had heard and seen, as it was told unto them." Luke 2:1-20 KJV

A Christmas Prayer

I might suggest that you begin each reading with this prayer ...

Dear Jesus,
I come to pause before You in this Christmas season. I bring You my—to-do list, my sharing, baking, and giving. I lay all of these down at Your feet—in order to quiet my heart, still my thoughts, and commune with You.

I bring You a simple offering, the gift of my praise, knowing everything that I have, am, or have to share—is from Your hand.

I pray that Your Spirit will fill me with joy and kindness, and that You'll encourage me to be observant to the needs around me.

This season can get so busy, God; it can fill up with many emotions and is easy to fill with earthly pursuits ... so I pray that You help me to focus my attention on You.

These moments of companionship, teach me to rely upon You— for strength, for love, for forgiveness. It's my desire that this time of meditation is like a crown—a symbol of worship to the Christ-Child, and to You, the King of Kings. Amen.

Happy, Meowy Christmas

"Glory to God in the highest heaven, and on earth peace to those on whom his favor rests." Luke 2:14 NIV

You might hear these words echo in the night air: In Italian, "Buon Natale;" In French, "Joyeuses fetes;" In Spanish, "Felices Fiestas;" In Hawaiian, "Mele Kalikimaka." In Japanese, "Merri Kurisumasu;" In some European nations, "Happy Christmas;" and in America, "Merry Christmas or Happy Holidays." Isn't it interesting that no matter our language— each nation has some form of greeting—for the Christmas/holiday season?

Nearing the time of Jesus' birth however, the greeting was this: *"Glory to God in the highest, and on earth peace, good will toward men (Luke 2:14 KJV)."* It was the proclamation of angels to shepherds in the hill country. It was to herald the Good News announcing Jesus' birth.

We begin our greetings toward one another in much the same way as the angels. Long before the 25th of December arrives, we make preparations—we buy gifts, decorate, send cards of invitation and greeting. We call out these cheerful words to passersby. We celebrate with loved ones and gather near and far, in person and in memory. This special and sacred holiday is both a world-wide event —and a personal experience—at the same time.

Cats, are not immune to its arrival. Somehow, even they seem to have more sparkle and joy, just as we do. As the lights come out and the carols begin, I pray that a sense of peace envelops your heart. For amidst the busyness and upcoming events, the planning and giving—may you also find room in your heart to give God glory.

A Purr of Prayer

Dear Lord, may love be the language of this Christmas season. May it be the communication of our hearts, of our homes, of our gift giving. And may we save space—in our schedules, in our resources, in our souls—to give You some meditation, some praise, some pause. We give You glory God—in Your highest heavenly realms, but in our minds, as well. We pray for peace to reign and joy to spread, like light. And may we share the Good News of Your coming ... to all mankind, to our families and friends. For in every land, it is You that we proclaim—as God, as Master, and King of All. Amen.

....

....

....

Happy, Meowy Christmas, and Blessed Paw-a-days—may the season of joy bring you, your family, friends (and furries) every good and perfect gift, from the Lord, above.

Angelic

She looked so angelic,
I had to check to see,
If she had sprouted,
A halo or feathered-wings.
She was the very image,
Of every perfect thing.
As she gazed forward,
And off to the side,
With sparkling beauties,
Green, and open-wide …
She made me wonder,
If by chance,
She was watching,
An angel's shimmering dance.
She took me to,
Another time and place,
Back in history,
To a manger-space.
An angel appeared,
Before a teen's sweet face,
Wrapping her,
In endless love and grace. …

… With a proclamation,
He would bring an annunciation,
From heaven, above.
"Mary, you will be with child,"
The Spirit will be reconciled;
"Do not be afraid,"
These are holy plans being made.
You are My beloved, chosen one,
Called upon,
To bear God's perfect Son.
And humbly this girl,
Gave her word;
With a song,
She agreed to all she heard.
She rejoiced,
She lifted praise.
Ever and always,
He will be named:
Immanuel,
Meaning, "God with us."

Mary was visited by an angel (Luke 1:26-35). Gabriel came to her at night to bring her tidings, the likes of which she had never heard before. She, a virgin, would bear a son. Yet, not just any child, but the very Son of God. The Holy Spirit would come upon her to make this declaration true. Willingly, she agreed to be the Lord's handmaiden, His servant (Luke 1:38).

But these circumstances—made her life, anything but—angelic. Imagine the questions that she had to answer. Some of which she could not fully understand or provide herself. And they would come from those closest to her, including Joseph, whom she was promised (or engaged) to. Ever think about the gossipers that must have hounded her? Ever think of those who would have ostracized her? Ever think of the villagers, her friends, who probably called her a liar, an impure girl and worse?

Yet, Jesus chose to be born in a way that would not be easy for this couple. He required them to journey—not just physically, but emotionally and spiritually—to a place that stretched them well beyond their years. This path would lead them to trust and a deeper faith than some will ever experience.

Angelic circumstances? No. But angelic faith, belief, trust, follow? Yes and Amen.

Jeepers was not always angelic in her behavior. She could give what Doug sometimes called—a withering glance—if she was displeased with something. But for the most part, she was cuddly, sweet, filled with purrs and praise. She was constantly meowing and chortling little songs through the house. Her joy couldn't be restrained; it was contagious. And I think Mary's was much the same. 'Cause when she received an *angelic visitation*, she was receptive, obedient, and willing to be God's handmaiden, His servant, His instrument.

A Purr of Prayer

Dear Lord, You may never give me an angelic visitation, but I am Your willing hands, Your willing heart to be used. I am Your willing servant. I am listening to Your voice. I am filled with a song of praise, and a heart full of joy. By faith, I will go where You lead. By trust, I will do what You will for me. And when I face opposition—I will draw close, like Mary—physically, emotionally, and spiritually. As Your child, I am grateful that You, the babe of the manger, became my sacrifice at the Cross. Amen.

Jesus is Immanuel, God with us. If we are His child, He is God—in us. May we be willing to share this love with those around us—with a servant's heart and attitude, as Mary, displayed.

Isaiah 7:14, Proverbs 3:5-6, 2 Corinthians 5:7

Room to pause in the Paw Print

....

....

....

"And in the sixth month the angel Gabriel was sent from God unto a city of Galilee, named Nazareth, To a virgin espoused to a man whose name was Joseph, of the house of David; and the virgin's name was Mary. And the angel came in unto her, and said, Hail, thou that art highly favored, the Lord is with thee: blessed art thou among women. And when she saw him, she was troubled at his saying, and cast in her mind what manner of salutation this should be. And the angel said unto her, Fear not, Mary: for thou hast found favor with God. And, behold, thou shalt conceive in thy womb, and bring forth a son, and shalt call his name JESUS. He shall be great, and shall be called the Son of the Highest: and the Lord God shall give unto him the throne of his father David: And he shall reign over the house of Jacob for ever; and of his kingdom there shall be no end. Then said Mary unto the angel, How shall this be, seeing I know not a man? And the angel answered and said unto her, The Holy Ghost shall come upon thee, and the power of the Highest shall overshadow thee: therefore also that holy thing which shall be born of thee shall be called the Son of God. ... And Mary said, Behold the handmaid of the Lord; be it unto me according to thy word.' And the angel departed from her." Luke 1:26-35, 38 KJV

Prayer of the Angel, Gabriel

Father God, Ruler of heaven and earth, tonight You send me to Mary as Your messenger. Grant me the words and gentle manner to reach this tender teen.

Turn her heart toward You, to absorb this truth in the way in which You intend (as a blessing). Help her to trust that You'll provide her—with joy, strength, peace and guidance—to endure the pain of childbirth, but also the false accusations, the gossip of neighbors who will judge her unfairly.

Give me Your power, O God, to shine Your light into her soul. And may all who read of this account, turn their eyes to Your miracle-working power.

Help Mary to be obedient to the sacred call upon her life, I pray. For both she and I have found favor in Your sight, mighty King. Amen.

<u>Your moment to pause</u>

Most of us have not had an angelic visitation, but God's Word and His voice give us guidance and direction in our day-to-day lives. Think about a time that required supernatural faith and then reflect on how God led you to obey Him.

....

....

<u>It's your turn to talk to God</u>

Lord, I thank You for Your faithfulness in showing me Your guidance in the area of:

....

....

By following You, I've learned to trust You in these ways:

1) ....

2) ....

3) ....

Anticipating Christmas

I began forming the foundations of my Christmas decorations around mid-November. I set up the support structure of my artsy tree, began putting the greenery on the bannister, placing lights and the flowers etc., before I add the ornaments. When under the tree, I noticed that I had a "Santa's helper." Her eyes were all aglow; her whiskers were alert with anticipation. Her paws were prepared for mischief.

16

Somehow, as soon as the deco. comes out, even our animals sense a change in the very atmosphere and become a little aware, a little more attuned to the happenings . And as I am wont to do, I began to ponder: Are we filled with anticipation ... as God's children, as this Holy season approaches? Now, my husband, family and friends, can tell you—that I am. But, are you?

Do you anticipate,
Not just the lights,
Not just the decorations,
And the gatherings?
But does your heart,
Wholly fill,
With the celebration to come?
Do you eagerly await,
The birthday,
Of baby Jesus?
Do you seek Him,
Like the wisemen?
Do you bring Him,
Offerings, from within ...

—a grateful mind,
—a loving attitude,
—a song of praise?
Do you ponder,
The beauty of this miracle?
That Jesus came to earth,
Humbly, to experience,
All that we do?
Do you come alive,
When you think that His purpose,
As a babe,
As a man,
Was to die upon a tree,
To save, you and me?

Jesus is the support system for the child of God. He is the reason that we have to celebrate—this life, this season, this very breath. So as you go about the baking, the decorating, the gathering, and sharing of packages all tied with bows ... and have fun with your furry-friends too ... I pray that you make the One Who came to earth and now reigns in heaven—the center of Christmas—as it approaches, and in every day of the coming year.

Happy Christmas

We had purchased this little set from an oriental market in downtown Oahu, HI. Just as the holiday season was about to begin, I spied it amongst the assortment of china, glassware and collectables, that were displayed in the housewares department. I was

drawn-in by the charm of the saying, "Happy Christmas." For this time of year seems to bring out the joy, bring out the merry, in most of mankind. And these kitties sure looked ready to spread some cheer!

There seems to be a little more kindness, a bit more gentleness, a few more acts of helpfulness in this beloved season. The very air seems to change—even in the warmer climate of Hawaii. The lights, the music, the special foods—the very celebration—filters into our homes, into our hearts—to make us, happy.

But just like Christmas is a temporary season, happiness—is a temporary emotion. What we really seek in our lives—is true peace and joy. These, come from having a relationship with the One—Whose birth we honor on this very special day. No matter how many gifts we purchase, how much love we give—Jesus is the gift—that puts the happy, puts the merry—puts the love, joy, peace, hope, grace—into our souls.

Happy Christmas! I hope you have a season that is filled with every good gift. But may you know the true joy that comes only from Jesus. 'Cause then, you will know joy, (and have all the Fruits of the Spirit—see below) everyday of the year.

Christmas celebrates the birth of Jesus, Who wishes to be born in your heart. When you accept the gift that He offers, you will find—more than happiness, more than good cheer—you will have an eternal hope, bliss, forgiveness, and grace. These are priceless, and the filter through which we share His love … in every market, in our families, with every gathering … with all mankind.

May the celebration of one tiny Babe, linger in your heart, to bring you ever-lasting joy!

Leaving a Paw Print
    Romans 15:13,
    Galatians 5:22-23

Cats and Christmas

Each of our three cats have adored Christmas. They have each taken delight when the tree and ornaments come out, the tissue starts to crackle, and the lights begin to shine. Each has reacted singularly and similarly to this holy time of year.

There's something about cats and Christmas,
It's like they can sense the special season in the air.
They love the rustle of unwrapping tissue,
Love, to watch the sparkle of the lights, so fair.
They seem to sit in wonder,
And gaze at the stars, icicles, and snowflakes.
Their eyes glisten like a little child's with fascination;
And like a child, they love to play from the time they wake.
They love the crinkle of paper,
They respond to everything that shines,
The texture of the trimmings and the bows.
They seem to be filled with the same joy that we are,
It's like they become illumined with the same sweet, glow.

Cats, remind us to cherish the simple things: the sights, the sounds, and the memories of the holiday season. Just like children, their delight helps us stop and behold the sweet joys and celebration of this treasured time. Just as their eyes twinkle with anticipation, I find I am filled with the same wonder—as I cherish the One Who was held in the manger.

In Luke 1:38, we are told that Mary declares herself to be "the Lord's servant." Here, is (part) of her song of praise unto the Lord: *"And Mary said: 'My soul glorifies the Lord and my spirit rejoices in God my Savior, for he has been mindful of the humble state of his servant. From now on all generations will call me blessed, for the Mighty One has done great things for me—holy is his name.'" Luke 1:46-49 NIV*

With such simple, child-like trust, this tender-aged-teen showed great trust in God. She already held the glow of His Spirit in her heart, in her soul. The spirit of Christmas—Christ's love—already filled her with a willingness to obey.

Mary's Prayer

Dear Lord,
How I exalt You. My spirit celebrates all that You have shared with me, Your humble servant-girl.

Thank You for taking notice of me, though I feel so ordinary. Great are You, O God; from generation to generation Your loving-kindness endures. I'm here to be Your vessel, Lord, and I long to serve and obey You.

When I hold the Christ-Child in my arms, my heart will swell with such love. I'm awestruck with the thought that as I will look into this wee one's eyes, I will be getting a glimpse of Your infinity, Your majesty and holiness. I'll ponder each moment of this journey, knowing You're giving me a gift—a special place in history, an honor among women, and a perspective to see You as the Light of the World. Amen.

Your moment to pause

How does Mary's song of exultation in Luke 2, teach us to bring our every concern, hope, dream and circumstance before God's heart and throne? How does knowing God as Confidant, teach us that we are seen, known and loved—perfectly—just as she was?

....

....

....

Your turn to talk to God

Dear Lord, like Mary, I feel ordinary. And while You arrived in an ordinary fashion, You were born to be love—to live out love—for all mankind. Teach me, how You want to use all of me.

I bring ....

....

for You to use—freely, willingly and obediently. Let my life, demonstrate that I love You, and that I too, have a servant's heart. Amen.

Wonder sparkled from Mary's eyes as she humbly accepted what would be a challenging role to fulfill. Yet her song, her light, her love of the Lord was her sweet glow.

So as Christmas draws nigh, I hope you will find the delight of the yuletide. I hope your heart grows lighter and that you are filled with a child-like joy. I pray that a sense of God's goodness and love enfolds you, and makes your soul purr with praise, as Mary's did. Adopt a little of a cat's sense of play, a little of their fascination, and let your eyes sparkle. No matter whether you are a pure-breed or feel like a shelter-pup—the King adores you, and that is what Christmas is all about.

Cats and "Signs"

Did you ever notice that cats are swift to notice, "signs?" What do I mean? Let's think about a few of our activities and how the feline responds. In our home, we usually exercise on our mini-trampolines—before—she gets her evening meal. So she, accompanies us downstairs. We joke, that she sees it as her necessary step, or sign, that food is on its way.

Another example would be if Doug and I are packing for a short get-a-way. As I pull the suitcase and our items together, each of our cats have come close. But when the bags start to get loaded in the car, their presence becomes scarce. Cats learn your routines, the rhythms of your home. They come to meet you when you return from running errands. Get out a gift to wrap or the Christmas decorations—and cats are usually in close proximity. Each of these things is like a sign to them ... that something is going on, something good is coming, or a possible treat is on the way.

The Bible is full of signs and wonders. Jesus gave these to us so that we would anticipate His Spirit's work, experience a quickening of the heart when we feel His presence. And they demonstrate that He is moving, shaping, in control of every happening in or around us.

When Jesus was born, Luke 2:12 tells us, that "this shall be a sign unto us." That the babe would be found in swaddling clothes and lying in a manger. God gave Mary a "sign"—an angel's appearance and greeting—to tell her that she would become the mother of the Christ-Child. God also gave such a sign to Joseph:

"These are the facts concerning the birth of Jesus Christ: His mother, Mary, was engaged to be married to Joseph. But while she was still a virgin she became pregnant by the Holy Spirit. Then Joseph, her fianceé, being a man of stern principle, decided to break the engagement but to do it quietly, as he didn't want to publicly disgrace her. As he lay awake considering this, he fell into a dream, and saw an angel standing beside him. 'Joseph, son of David,' the angel said, 'don't hesitate to take Mary as your wife! For the child within her has been conceived by the Holy Spirit. And she will have a Son, and you shall name him Jesus (meaning 'Savior'), for he will save his people from their sins. This will fulfill God's message through his prophets —Listen! The virgin shall conceive a child! She shall give birth to a Son, and he shall be called 'Emmanuel' (meaning 'God is with us').' When Joseph awoke, he did as the angel commanded and brought Mary home to be his wife, but she remained a virgin until her Son was born; and Joseph named him 'Jesus.'" Matthew 1:18-25 (TLB)

The Old Testament is filled with signs, from a burning bush in Exodus, to a cloud and pillar of fire as traveling companions.

During His ministry ... Jesus gave many signs as He performed miracles. He did these so that we would not miss Him. He gave signs to demonstrate His power, authority, and divinity (while at the same time, He was fully human.)

What about the ultimate sign—creation? Romans 1:20, tells us that no one has/will have an excuse for not seeing God because He speaks, universally, through all that He's made. His love, beauty, and creativity are on display, daily.

And we are given these signs so that we are on the look-out for His second coming.

Here's an interesting Bible Study: try to find examples of "signs" in Scripture ... then think about how you would respond if you were present. Now pause, and view them from both the historical and personal perspective—by taking time to note your observations. How is Jesus trying to speak to you through these examples?

....

....

....

....

Prayer of Joseph

Dear Jehovah,

An angel came to me tonight in a dream. He brought the tidings that Mary, my sweet fiancée Mary, is with child. Yet You know we have lived purely before You. Grant me faith to believe that this conception is by Your divine power, for Your miraculous purpose.

I will be obedient to this calling and take her as my wife as You've directed. I will trust our journey to Your sovereignty and care. Teach us, Lord, to trust You in the days ahead—through the doubts, in spite of our fears. And grant us courage to endure false whispers, so that we hear only Your voice and follow where You lead. Amen.

Your moment to Pause

In what area is God asking for your trust, your belief in this Christmas season? In what space is He asking you to lay aside your expectations, in order to take up His promise and obey? Through what hardship has God safely delivered, you?

....

....

....

It's your turn to talk to Jehovah

Dear Lord, I am feeling fear in the area of:

....

....

....

but I am praying that You will turn it to faith, for I am trusting ... that as You were God to Joseph, You will guide my steps, today.

Advent, means the "arrival or coming" of something or someone, that is "especially important." It is the time on our calendars that marks the four Sundays prior to Christmas. It is the celebration leading up to the arrival of the Baby Jesus; but it also symbolically looks ahead to the second coming of Christ.

Advent itself, began as early as 380 AD; France, and Spain are noted as the originators of the ritual, while Germany introduced the custom of using the Advent Wreath and the lighting of candles, which many churches have adopted as part of this celebration. Modern Advent, is attributed to Rome, from the late 6th or early 7th century. It is a custom, cherished, that has spread throughout the world. But to me, Advent, signifies a sense of anticipation. For on both counts—the Nativity, (the Birth of Jesus) and His second coming—were, and are, the events that we long for.

The Message of Advent

Each week, a new candle is lit, to represent various gifts and attributes of God's Spirit. Hope, Love, Joy and Peace, are proclaimed via a pictorial illustration of a wreath or freeform candle-lighting ceremony. So today, I thought I would take a minute to encourage you … with some promises for each of these elements.

Hope

Isaiah 40:31	1 Peter 1:3-5
Jeremiah 29:11	Psalm 147:11
Romans 15:13	Romans 5:5

Joy
1 Thessalonians 5:16-18
Psalm 16:11
Isaiah 61:10
3 John 1:4
Zephaniah 3:17

Peace
Numbers 6:24-26
John 14:27
Psalm 4:8
Isaiah 26:3
Isaiah 52:7
Psalm 29:11
Luke 2:14

Love
John 3:16-17
1 John 4:7
1 John 4:10
2 Thessalonians 3:5
Psalm 136:2-3
Romans 8:38-39
Galatians 5:22-23

Christ Alone
John 14:6
1 Timothy 2:5-6
Acts 4:12
1 Peter 2:24
2 Corinthians 5:17
Revelation 1:8

May each week in this procession of candle lighting, be not just a symbol, but bring true illumination to your heart. For the babe, Jesus —is the King of Kings and Lord of Lords. He rules and reigns. He was, and is, and is to come. And the message of Advent is not simply an act of lighting candles 'round a display—but it is an opportunity to experience the circle of God's amazing love—encompassing all that we do and give—in His Holy season. I hope you take time to look up these promises, for they are filled with the attributes of His Spirit. And I pray that this meditation will draw your heart closer to our God and Father.

An Advent Prayer

Oh Lord,
May Hope,
Rise in our hearts,
To fill our souls with Joy—
Till it overflows,
Into Peace.
May we radiate,
The Love of Christ,
To everyone we meet,
In this Holy Season!

And may You,
Be the Center,
Of all that we say,
Do, share, or give,
We pray.
For this is to have an advent,
An awakening,
Of You.
Amen.

We loved catching Muffin, resting within the wreath that was about to hung on the front door. Cat's hearts seem to beat a little faster—as if they know "it's time" for their home to "come alive." All three of ours have joined-in, in the festivity making.

We have had tree-climbers, ornaments mistaken for their toys, and "helpers" when gifts were wrapped and tied with bows. Cats are much like children in this regard. They seem to have an innate excitement that rises as the halls are decked and the carols begin to ring through the air.

"In preparation of Jesus birth, Caesar Augustus, issued a decree that a census should be taken of the entire Roman world. This was the first census that took place while Quirinius was governor of Syria. And everyone went to his own town to register. So Joseph also went up from the town of Nazareth in Galilee to Judea, to Betlehem the town of David, because he belonged to the house and line of David. He went there to register with Mary, who was pledged to be married to him and was expecting a child. While they were there, the time came for the baby to be born, and she gave birth to her firstborn, a son. She wrapped him in cloths and placed him in a manger, because there was no room for them in the inn." Luke 2:1-7 NIV

Can you imagine Mary's mix of emotions as "her time" came near? The uncertainty, excitement, and wonderment must have all combined in an amazing way as God's Spirit gently and joyfully guided her path. Jesus includes all of mankind in this invitation to seek Him.

May a sense of anticipation permeate your heart, not just in December, but all throughout the year. For though the lights and the gifts come out for only a season—Jesus' love came down from heaven to a manger stall, where even the animals of the pasture gathered 'round to give Him adoration. Perhaps that is why all of His creatures ... respond so sweetly and dearly, to this time of year. Could it be that the Lord places a certain "knowing" or awareness in their little hearts ... in ours, that makes everything, everyone ... "come alive" ... in His Holy presence, at Christmas?

Let us "come alive" to be the light of Christmas, so that all the world wants to know, what gives us our "sparkle." It's time! Everyday!

Happy, Merry
Christmas, and
Blessed Paw-a-Days

In an earlier entry, I introduced you to the greeting: "Happy Christmas." It actually predates the use of "Merry Christmas," which became widely used in the 18th and 19th century.

"Happy Christmas" originated in England, and is still used as a holiday blessing in places like Hawaii, along with a number of European nations. Queen Elizabeth II is credited for the phrase which she used in her annual, national broadcasts.

Many Christians have begun a campaign-of-sorts that say that it is wrong to say "Happy Holidays." I understand their meaning. They feel that to not say, "Merry Christmas," may take away from the reverence of this Holy Day.

But here is another way to see this. First of all, there *are* multiple holidays within November, December and January. So it is not exactly inaccurate to use this more generic greeting. Second, the Lord looks at the heart and knows that to use a simple phrase, is not taking anything away from Him, His glory, or the significance of this beauty of His birth.

If we love the Lord and give Him adoration in our hearts, He is praised. Third, it may, in some cases, actually be a bridge-builder with those of other faiths. Ever think of that?

Personally, I use each of these in varying circumstances. I find Happy Christmas, to hold a charm and simplicity which has a certain appeal. Merry Christmas, implies that Christ is first in my life (which He is) and that I am wishing everyone around me, a blessing. When we say Happy Holidays, we are being inclusive or respectful to those who do not share our beliefs or faith, which may in fact, draw them to us and ultimately, to Him.

Why is this important? Because the very foundation of the Christmas story—the birth and arrival of Jesus—was/is love. So no matter our greeting—our purpose is to perpetuate the blessings of kindness, hope, and joy, to everyone around us. This, should be our concern and the meditation of our heart.

We should never—take anything away from God's glory; but we should never exclude anyone—from coming to know Him—either. The message of our greeting and of our hearts, should be to extend His grace, His mercy, His goodness—so that others will be drawn—to Him, to His saving power—especially, at this most precious time of year.

Happy, Merry Christmas. May your paws (pause), and may you purr (bring some praise) to Jesus during this Holy Holiday Season! And

may you be blessed beyond measure, no matter which greeting you choose, because the Babe of the Manger is the King of All. And He loves you, blessedly!

The Star of Bethlehem

In our home—light, began at the ceiling, to touch the tree. It danced 'round and 'round, until it glistened from Jeepers' eyes. The Star of Bethlehem shone o'er the manger onto Jesus, Who was the Light of the World. His indwelling Spirit places a glow in us that illumines not just our souls, but serves as a lantern unto our path, and reflects God's love to those around us.

The Moravian Star,
Glowed above the tree.
Lights, will soon dance,
Twinkling, as if with glee.
Jeepers, sits 'neath the limbs,
With bright, shining eyes,
As if she knows that the season,
Is for the seeking, the wise.
Do you behold the Holy Star of Bethlehem?
Do you search for the Light of the World?
Do you seek,
As the Wisemen, did ...
The Messiah, the Babe, King, Priceless Pearl?
Oh God,
As gifts circle the evergreen,
May we be reminded,
Of the manger scene.
For Your humble birth,
Your very entrance into earth ...
Was the illumination;
It was the proclamation,
The Star of Heaven,
Shines forevermore.
May the ember of hope,
Be like a lantern of peace,
Touching everywhere,
That we go,
To be released.
For when we sit,
Or when we rise,
Sleep or wake,
To open our eyes,
May You be the light,
Within our souls.

Love is a circle, that shines ever bright. Its Source is the Holy One, Jesus. May every light of the Christmas season, remind you that He is the Way, the One Who shines peace, out of the darkness. May each one of us, seek ... to worship, Jesus, the Babe, the King.

"Jesus was born in Bethlehem in Judea, during the reign of King Herod. About that time some wise men from eastern lands arrived in Jerusalem, asking, 'Where is the newborn king of the Jews? We saw his star as it rose, and we have come to worship him.' ... When they saw the star, they were filled with joy! They entered the house and saw the child with his mother, Mary, and they bowed down and worshiped him. Then they opened their treasure chests and gave him gifts of gold, frankincense, and myrrh. When it was time to leave, they returned to their own country by another route, for God had warned them in a dream not to return to Herod."
Matthew 2:1-2, 10-12 NLT

The Moravian Star was made to be a representation of the Star of Bethlehem. Both the candles which were originally used on Christmas trees, and the electric lights that we now use today—draw our eye upward. Our Light came as a holy Babe wrapped in humanity—to point us to the love and gift—Jesus.

Prayer of the Star

O Creator, how majestic You are to honor me this night. You're giving me more radiance and greater iridescence than ever before ... and I am focusing this splendor on the little town of Bethlehem, on the manger-scene, the place of Your birth.

How glad I am to be part of Your celebration! How my light is like a gift of anointing to Your holy head. How blessed I feel to lead the wisemen to You, so that they can bring You gifts and adoration. How awesome it feels to shine for Your glory. I'm about to explode with joy, unspeakable—communicated silently, brightly—to all the world with the anticipated message: "Jesus has arrived!" Amen.

Your moment to pause

The stars, the heavens declare the glory of God, nightly. How does their appearing, fill you with awe? How might you have felt as this star, this 'orb, highlighted not only the birthplace, but the very celebration of Jesus, the Messiah?

....

....

....

Your turn to talk to Jesus

I come like the star, filled with reverence. I worship You as the Light of the World, the light of my heart, the light of ... (fill in the blanks with your greatest need, concern, dream, etc.)

....

....

....

Amen.

"Look up into the heavens! Who created all these stars? As a shepherd leads his sheep, calling each by its pet name, and counts them to see that none are lost or strayed, so God does with stars and planets!"
Isaiah 40:26 TLB

The Light Ride

One of our Christmas traditions is to take a night or two (at least) in the holiday season to drive around and view the lights/decorations. And on one of those excursions each year, I swaddle our cat and take he/she along. Pictured, is Tiger Lily, on one such wintery night.

While our other cats have liked to cuddle, she doesn't enjoy that so much as simply being near. We call her our "penny pup." She's usually in close proximity, but doesn't normally curl up in our lap, etc. So when I include her on our light-viewing, I get the pleasure of hugging her—meaning, that she allows it without fuss, wiggling or protest. For some reason, when we are in a car (a long or short journey), she seems to enjoy the comfort of my arms, the affection and close communion of being held.

Christmas brings many emotions—to cats, and we humans, alike. What brings joy to one person, brings painful memories to another. It's a time of gathering for some, loneliness for others. It's a time of celebration to one family, and a reminder of separation, divorce, or grief to another. But no matter where we find ourselves—Jesus is the One Who longs to hold us close, soothe our fears, bring us comfort and give us His gracious attention. He wants to shine His light on your heart, your mind, and your circumstances.

So whether you already share in our tradition or want to adopt it … whether you decide to go for a Christmas light-viewing drive for the first time … or just need to know that you are loved … look into the eyes of the Savior. The One Who came as a swaddled infant, grew to become the light of every heart. Today, He's the risen King Who illuminates the corridors of heaven.

Tilly enjoys being held closely as we sing carols and watch the twinkling lights from the car windows. Jesus' eyes are shining with affection for you. Come, get yourself embraced! Come, find healing and joy in God's loving arms of grace.

Lord, please make Yourself known to me this Christmas. Help me to feel Your nearness, no matter how near or far I have to travel, and no matter what my circumstances bring. Amen.

The light-ride, brings a glow to our hearts while wrapping us in the reminder of God's perfect embrace.

Looking Up in Wonder

When we get snow, Tiger Lily is at the door waiting to come outside with me to enjoy it. She loves to taste it, play in it, and seems to get lost in the beauty of its magical arrival and disappearance.

On this particular day, her pose reminded me of the shepherds looking for the first sighting of the star of Bethlehem. Her expression almost seems to say, "I see something that's visible *only* to the seeking." Well Tilly, my heart joins yours in this watchful attitude. I want to see the miracle of Jesus too.

A Purr of Prayer

Dear Lord, may we have a "looking up in wonder" type of spirit, not just at Christmas, but toward Your Son, always. May You show us the unseen things of heaven, so that we believe a little more strongly in Your divine power and nature that is displayed on earth everyday. Amen.

"Looking up in wonder" keeps our eyes trained on our Master.

"Great are the works of the Lord; they are pondered by all who delight in them." Psalm 111:2 NIV

With Ribbons and Bows

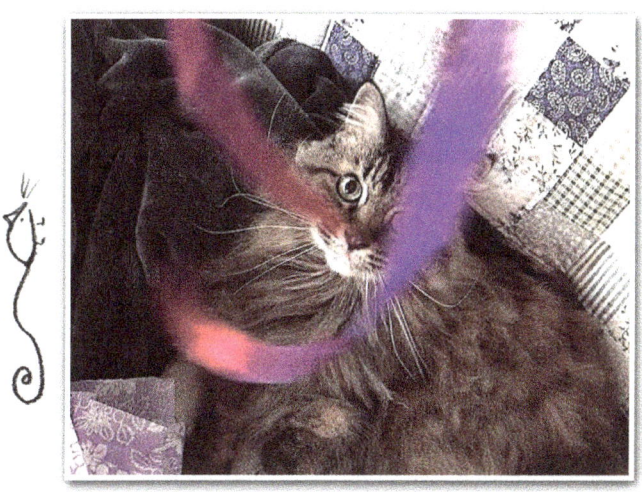

I loved catching a glimpse of Tiger Lily through these fluttering ribbons as we played with her. In the foreground, you can see a bit of tissue that goes with a gift that these came from. Cats seem to be as amazingly content with the outside wrappings of packages as they are with the gift itself. And I thought this was an interesting topic to explore, in reference to how God views the gifts He gives us.

- Jesus is more concerned with the gift of life that He gave us than by how we appear. Do we spend more time on our internal selves than on our external appearance, and do we value His opinion over the thoughts/words of others?
- Our heavenly Father is concerned with our attitude: Are we grateful for Who He is? And all the ways He cares for us, and how He provides for our needs?
- The Lord is looking for our heart's willingness to let Him lead our lives. Are we submitted to His Will?
- God is looking for a spirit of contentment in us. Do we rely upon Him for our joy, strength, hope, and trust that His ways are best?
- Do we share our time, talents, and of our resources with Him and others?

Ribbons and bows became the focus of Tilly; she's a cat after all. But Jesus wants to take us deeper than the superficial things of earth. If we want to serve Him, (and Christmastime holds so many opportunities) then, we sometimes need to look beyond the outer packaging—and remember that every soul needs the love of Jesus. This helps us to share our faith and perhaps encourage someone to see themselves with fresh eyes—as the gift God means for them to be to the world. To give that gift … is priceless!

Leaving a Paw Print
      1 Samuel 16:7, Psalm 139:14, Proverbs 3:5-6,
      1 Thessalonians 5:11, 1 Timothy 6:6

Room to pause in the Paw Print

....

....

....

Within the Wrappings

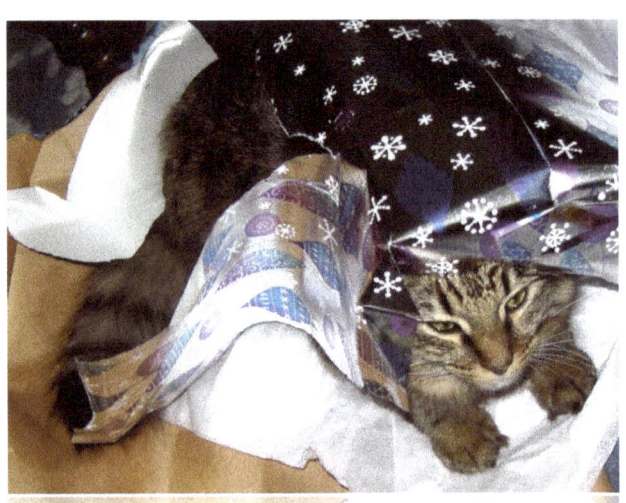

If you have a cat,
Then you probably know this is true …
When you open a gift,
This, is exactly what they do …
They love to hide,
In the wrappings;
They love to play,
With the tissue and the bows.

They delight as much,
In the outer trimmings,
As whatever was held inside.

And just as Tiger Lily,
Had a little fun on Christmas day,
She reminded me,
That she is a gift,
Everyday.

Jesus came to earth to be laid in a manger—a feeding trough. He was wrapped in the simplest of swaddling clothes. Yet heaven shone down brilliantly, wrapping Him in its glorious light. Wisemen, brought Him gifts to show their adoration. For what was contained in the cradle at Bethlehem—*was* the gift.

Jesus, remains so to all mankind, everyday. But we must open our hearts. We must unwrap our sacredly held secrets, be vulnerable and expose our deepest need—for Him. We must be undone, recognizing that our outer appearance is not enough, until every part of us has been cleansed by His love and grace.

Come under the covering,
Of God's mercy.
Open the tender places,
Of your heart.
Humbly, wholly, yield,
And you will discover that Jesus,
Came to earth, simply.
He is approachable …

… He was held in a manger,
So that every living thing,
Would know that the King,
Brought the gift of love,
To the world.
He is the gift,
Everyday,
To everyone.

Jesus, left the beauty and wrappings of heaven to be enrobed in humanity. This, was so that His saving blood would purify all (every single person) who calls upon His name. Simply, purely, He is the gift. Open your heart, unwrap His grace. For this is where He openly resides, in our center, right where His Spirit comes to dwell.

Within the wrappings of swaddling clothes—was a baby, a sacrifice, a King, and a gift. Have you opened your heart? Have you made room, to adore Him?

....

....

....

Leaving a Paw Print   John 1:14, Galatians 4:4

Prayer of the Wisemen

Dear Adonai,

We've followed a glorious star to find You and the location of Your birthplace. We've met Your delightful mother, Mary, and earthly papa, Joseph. We've seen the humble place where You lay Your head and how You've come to earth to dwell among mankind. And though 'tis but a stable-scene, it's filled with holiness and reverence. We come, bowing before You as the Messiah and Lord of All.

Jesus, how amazing that You would use us, the simple seekers of Your truth, to be Your first Disciples, allowing us to share Your Good News!

We come bearing earthly gifts of gold, frankincense and myrrh, which symbolize Your heavenly worth and renown. And we come, with adoration and praise in our hearts, wanting to know You as Savior.

Come, Jesus, be the gift of our lives and grant us words to share of this miracle that we've witnessed firsthand. Amen.

Your moment to pause

The wisemen brought earthly treasure to honor a divine God, the Christ-Child. These were their highest offerings to convey the love of their hearts. What is God asking of you? What is He asking you to give? What is the Lord asking you to share in this Christmas season? What is He asking you to lay down at His feet? Have you offered Him the room to become Your Lord, Savior and Guide?

....

....

....

....

Your turn to talk to God

Dear Adonai, I bring my heart as a humble gift of worship. Teach me how to honor You, above all else. Show me any area where You do not hold first place. I will follow You in ...

....

.... as an act of adoration and praise. Amen.

The Gift of Giving

I was assembling and wrapping a few presents for Christmas when suddenly, I noticed that …

I have a little furry elf,
Who shows up around Christmastime.
She hears the sound of paper and tissue,
And up onto the table she climbs.
She offers her "paws of assistance,"
And finds ribbon with which to play …
Tilly loves to investigate,
Anything, having to do with this special day!

One of the joys of Christmas is sharing gifts with friends and loved ones. It is a way to express love, kindness, and that we are thinking of them in this holy season. I love that our cats have each taken delight in this process. Sometimes, they offer a little too much help. But they seem to take as much joy as I do when it comes to giving.

And Jesus—is our supreme example of a life offered—in giving of Himself. He came to offer us love, hope, grace, joy, and peace. He's our Good Shepherd, our Helper, our strength, and the One Who fills us—in order to be a blessing to others.

So whether you give many or few gifts this holiday season, send cards, give monetary gifts to loved ones or donations to a charity, may the love of Jesus be your motivation. May His Spirit be your help and source of strength. And may you be filled with joy from your generosity. For in sharing of ourselves, we are most like Jesus.

"Give to others, and God will give to you. Indeed, you will receive a full measure, a generous helping, poured into your hands—all that you can hold. The measure you use for others is the one that God will use for you."
Luke 6:38 GNT

There was Exultation

There was the echo of praise,
In Mary's pondering heart.

There was a silent star,
That lit the velvety sky.
There were shepherds in the field,
Drawing nigh.
There were wisemen,
Seeking,
To come adore and bow,
Before the Christ-child …
Can you hear,
His cry of life, now?

There was the echo of praise,
In Mary's pondering heart.

There was a choir of angels,
Joined to offer God glory.
In the highest realms of heaven,
To the furtherest reaches of earth,
They declare His story.
There was the lowing of cattle,
And the cooing of doves;
There was a holy orchestration,
In creation, below, and above.
There was joy, unspeakable,
In Bethlehem-town,
That still rises to give the King,
His great renown.

There was the echo of praise,
In Mary's pondering heart.

There was a spirit of exultation surrounding every part of Jesus' birth. Angels announced His arrival and sang over Him as an anointing of worship. Creation—a star, mankind, even animals— were present to offer adoration. He was heralded with gifts of God's good earth.

Luke 2:13-20 (NIV), gives us this summary: *"Suddenly a great company of the heavenly host appeared with the angel, praising God and saying, 'Glory to God in the highest heaven, and on earth peace to those on whom his favor rests.' When the angels had left them and gone into heaven, the shepherds said to one another, 'Let's go to Bethlehem and see this thing that has happened, which the Lord has told us about.' So they hurried off and found Mary and Joseph, and the baby, who was lying in the manger. …*

… When they had seen him, they spread the word concerning what had been told them about this child, and all who heard it were amazed at what the shepherds said to them. But Mary treasured up all these things and pondered them in her heart. The shepherds returned, glorifying and praising God for all the things they had heard and seen, which were just as they had been told."

I love how verse 19 tells us that Mary "treasured" these things and "pondered" them in her heart. In other words, she was filled with a holy exultation. She gave God her adoration.

So now it's your turn to do likewise: First of all, I'd like for you to immerse yourself into the scenes of Luke 2. Imagine yourself at an angel's appearing. Envision the multitude of heavenly hosts proclaiming "Glory to God in the highest." Picture the Babe, Jesus, giving His first piercing cry to declare life on earth. Behold Mary, holding Him in her arms and weeping over all that had transpired, and all that was to come. Then form your own exultation.

....

....

....

Then, think of something in your modern-day life that is worthy of treasuring, pondering. How has God provided for you this year? How has He shown Himself to be Lord and King of an event or circumstance? In what way can you simply ponder His holiness? Now, form a prayer or listing of your exultation from this perspective.

....

....

....

....

....

Finally, how do your ideas/meditations relate? How do they differ? Do you have *the echo of praise in your pondering heart*?

....

....

....

Might there have been a kitten,
Near the manger,
Of the Christ-Child?
Might there have been a sweet,
Little—purr, pad, meow?
Might a furry-one,
Have been present,
In the stable yard …
Along with the lowing cattle,
The bleating lambs,
And the cooing doves?

"Yahweh, You are my God; I will exalt You. I will praise Your name, for You have accomplished wonders, plans formed long ago, with perfect faithfulness." Isaiah 25:1 HCSB

Can your imagination conjure the tiny Babe having such a serenade? Did the animals who surrounded the baby Jesus, join with Mary to sing such a perfect lullaby? For as she pondered the events that had taken place over the months preceding her son's birth—I can almost hear her hum-of-praise—rising into the starry canopy, above her head.

I can envision Mary singing as the animals gathered 'round the manger. It makes me ponder whether she was brought back to the scene again and again. Perhaps the very song that begins the Christmas story (in Luke 1), is the same one that all of God's creations sang—to give Him honor on this Holy Night.

Oh how the kitten,
The lamb, the dove,
The donkey, the oxen,
The calf, the lamb …
May have joined-in,
With a song of praise.
It must have sounded,
Like angels in the corridors, above;
Oh God, how wondrous,
Are Your, amazing ways.

It was a Holy Night that first Christmas. It remains so, to this day. And while including a kitten in this sacred scene is a flight-of-fancy (purely imagination on my part), the setting of Jesus' birth was a simple wooden manger. He was born in a stable that was part of an inn. So there would have been animals on the premises which probably included cows. I could not fathom that an inn would not have had their own milk supply … so thus, a kitten or two … may not have been far behind!

May this whimsical piece—bring your heart a little joy and delight—which is the very purpose of the Christ-Child. He came to bring the message of love to all mankind. It was a Holy Night when He was born!

What Kind of Gift?

This is our feline, checking out a present that we got for her. If you were to caption it, it might say: "What kind of gift—is this?" She might prefer the real thing (a live mouse), but we wouldn't!

Turns out, it was a gift for her to chase, but because these mice make a squeaking sound, they were a gift to us also. You see, when she misbehaves, we squeeze one of them to deter her from getting into something.

Ever get a gift that you wondered something similar? Ever receive something that was way too big? Broken, chipped? Or that had been clearly regifted? How did you feel? Did you know that is not the heart of God, being expressed?

Jesus, is the perfect gift to share in this holy season. He fits every heart, meets every need. He made each of us uniquely and celebrates us, thusly. He died for each one of us, yet has no favorites; we are each precious in His sight. And He offers each of us the same opportunity to except His offer of grace, forgiveness, and Salvation.

What kind of gift was Jesus, the Babe? A humble offering to the world, so that we might know God longs to meet us where we are. What kind of gift is Jesus of the Cross? The precious One Who gave His life for us, to prove that he gives us worth, value, and that He loves us, unconditionally. What kind of gift is offered? Salvation—faith in the One Who gives us eternal life and the gift of faith to be shared. What kind of gift do we have to offer Him? Our obedience, praise, and giving His presence away, in the way that we live.

The best gift we can ever receive—is Jesus. The best gift we can ever share or give—Jesus.

Leaving a Paw Print

> 2 Corinthians 9:15, 2 Timothy 1:9, James 1:17,
> Matthew 7:11, 1 Peter 4:10-11

Room to pause in the Paw Print

....
....
....

Nestled

Our kitten was nestled,
All snug in our bed,
I wondered if visions,
Of the Christ-Child,
Filled her sweet head.

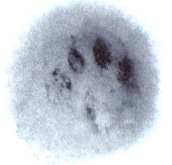

For when Jesus was born, He was wrapped in swaddling clothes, but His bed was not quite as cozy as Tilly's. He was born in a stable, since the inn was full. He was born with the lowing of cattle, joining Mary's lullaby. And He was born, not with the splendor that He deserved, but in the company of ordinary shepherds who traveled to meet and worship Him.

This is a great message to our hearts.
- God came wrapped in humanity, so He would identify with our humanness (John 1:14).
- He came in a divine way (born to a virgin via a miracle) but must be sought to be found (Isaiah 7:14).
- He is available to every one of every race, occupation, social standing, etc. (John 3:16-17).
- We must make room for Him, invite Him into our hearts, if He is to be our Lord and Savior (Revelation 3:20).

A Purr of Prayer

Dear Jesus, thank You for coming to earth to give us peace, and for reaching out to one and all. Thank You for being born with the purpose of being our sacrificial Lamb and for rising again as the King of Kings to reign forevermore. You came so that we can be nestled in Your hand, in Your care, for all eternity. I'm willingly making room for You in my heart, to be my Lord and Savior. Amen.

Room for your Purr of Prayer

....

....

....

No Vacancy

When Tiger Lily was a wee kitten, she used to share my pillow. Each night she would cuddle-up, to sleep. It was so precious! But then, she began to grow; she put on weight and length. I like to say that "she learned how to sprawl." Soon, she took over the whole space and left no room for my head. I felt like my pillow—had "no vacancy."

Well, another wee tike had this same issue. Jesus came into the world as a babe. Mary and Joseph had traveled a great distance to obey the law of the land—to come and "be counted" as there was a census being taken (Luke 2:1-6). When they arrived in Bethlehem, the inn had no room. "No vacancy" might as well as have hung from the shingle, as the owners had only the stable to offer. And the little Lord Jesus had only an animal's feeding trough as His bed.

"And she brought forth her firstborn son, and wrapped him in swaddling clothes, and laid him in a manger; because there was no room for them in the inn." Luke 2:7 KJV

Such lowly provisions for the Babe, the King. Yet this One Who was prophesied about, would come humbly to be the greatest gift the world has ever known. His renown would be proclaimed by a star. He may have arrived more than 2000 years ago, but the wise, still seek Him. The brave, still make room for Him.

And in this holy season, I pray that you cuddle-up to sleep, and to remember the Christ-Child. Jesus made you uniquely, loves you completely, and wants to dwell in your heart for all time.

Come grow with Jesus. Make room. Give Him an invitation. Let Him know that your heart has a vacancy and He will be Your Lord. That's the greatest gift you can receive (to give yourself) this Christmas. Then sprawl at His feet, worship, adore. Get to know this Jesus, as a babe, as King, as Abba Daddy. For no one did more to show you that He has room in His kingdom, for you.

Refreshment

The setting? We had gone on a short get-away. Doug and I went to purchase a few essentials after checking in to the motel, and came back to find this scene. Tilly had made herself "at home."

Cats can make themselves comfy in almost any space. Even when traveling, they seem to find the coziest spot. We loved finding Tilly reclining in the sunshine that washed over the bed on this wintery afternoon. She was seeking its warmth, the light that cascaded from the window. She made it look easy to relax after a long drive.

Sometimes the holiday season can leave us feeling in need of a respite. Our schedules can get so busy that we often need to remind ourselves to stop and rest, to make room, to set aside time to meet with the One Who is our Source of strength, peace, and solace. These moments, spent with the Son—warm us, replenish us, and fill us with the energy to be His love to those around us.

"Come to me, all you who are weary and burdened, and I will give you rest. Take my yoke upon you and learn from me, for I am gentle and humble in heart, and you will find rest for your souls. For my yoke is easy and my burden is light." Matthew 11:28-30 NIV

The greatest sense of refreshment that we can ever find, is when we recline at the feet of Jesus. When we are "at home" in His presence, He is "at home"—to fill us, restore us, and fill us—with everything that we need to obey, give, and share of His good gifts.

Leaving a Paw Print

Exodus 33:14, Isaiah 26:3, Romans 15:32

Awe

I love the look of awe,
That seems to brighten,
Cat's faces,
As the lights and decorations,
Come out,
At Christmas time.
I adore the sparkle,
In their eyes,
Like sweet anticipation.
This glow from within,
Shines all around,
And lightens every heart,
With love that, abounds.

There is something about this special season when everything begins to glow that reminds me of "awe." It is in the eyes of children, on every street corner, and shines from every heart that knows Jesus, as Lord. This "sparkle" is a sign of our love for our Creator; it is the visible symbol of adoration.

It reminds me of the reaction of the shepherds, when an angel of the Lord appeared to them: *"In the same region there were some shepherds staying out in the fields and keeping watch over their flock by night. And an angel of the Lord suddenly stood before them, and the glory of the Lord shone around them; and they were terribly frightened. But the angel said to them, 'Do not be afraid; for behold, I bring you good news of great joy which will be for all the people; for today in the city of David there has been born for you a Savior, who is Christ the Lord. This will be a sign for you: you will find a baby wrapped in cloths and lying in a manger.' And suddenly there appeared with the angel a multitude of the heavenly host praising God and saying, 'Glory to God in the highest, and on earth peace among men with whom He is pleased.'"* Luke 2:8-14 NASB

What news! How their hearts must have been filled with amazement at the words that were spoken to them. And the angel, gave these men not only a divine sign in his very appearance, but told them where and how to find the Babe. Then, this angel was joined by a host of angelic beings that came proclaiming praise and giving glory unto Jesus—the One, Whom they were seeking.

Do you have,
A look of awe,
To brighten your countenance?
Does your soul purely shine,
With the Spirit's, light?
For if we worship Jesus,
Then the glow of His presence,
Will lighten every space,
With His love,
To abound.

Awe, means to reverence, respect, or to have a sense of wonder at a thing/person's beauty. It can also mean to admire, or give honor, to those in authority.

"Are there any gods like you, Lord? No! There are no gods like you. You are wonderfully holy. You are amazingly powerful. You do great miracles." Exodus 15:11 ICB

Prayer of the Shepherds

Lord God, here we were, simple shepherds in the fields tending our lambs and wee ewes. When suddenly, above our heads an angel appeared to tell us of Your birth. Then, he was joined by a multitude of these heavenly beings. In the night sky, they seemed to glow.

Then, their voices joined in song in a chorus-like chant that seemed to echo across the landscape: "Glory to God in the highest and on earth peace, good will toward all men." In its repeating, we could not help but join in with the anthem raised unto You.

Even the lambs seemed to look-up with a sense of wonderment reflected in their eyes. Our hearts were full that night! For You had come to us—those that our neighbors often forgot. You spoke Your message of hope to our hearts—while we kept the night watch. And You brought a declaration to all mankind, while we were still enough to behold Your glory. What a night that was, indeed! Amen.

Your moment to pause

Do you sometimes feel overlooked in your job, in your church, in your family? God knows you. He sees you. He wants to speak to you as He did to the simple shepherds in the field. If you will open His Word, He will come to you. If you pray to Him, He'll listen and respond.

Will you commit to taking time each day to humbling yourself before Him? And to proclaim Him as the Lord of Your life? In what ways can you convey that you have submitted your heart to the Creator?

....

....

Your turn to talk to God

Dear Lord, You are the Good Shepherd, I am your little lamb. I feel lost and in need of Your peace for:

....

....

I commit to including You in every part of my day—my job/school, my parenting/grand-parenting, my gardening, my serving, my comings and goings. And as You teach me more of Your ways, I will give You glory and share Your love with those around me. Amen.

As the cats sit and gaze at the Christmas lights, their expressions remind me of how we should look, when we simply "think" about Jesus. This is how our countenances should appear when we pray, when we praise, when we interact with our Holy Lord. For if we have reverence in our hearts, we surrender all we are to His care. His love will purely shine from the soul with light not just at Christmas, but everyday.

Glory to God in the highest! It is our proclamation at any time, to give our great God, praise!

They're so Tempting

If asked to choose a caption,
For the look on kitty's face,
As she sits neath the Christmas tree,
Under limbs decorated with icy lace …
One might say,
"They're so tempting,"
These ornaments,
Before her eyes.
Oh, how they dangle,
For sure, they tantalize.

What's in your path;
What is holding your gaze?
What thing or place,
Draws your interest into its space?
What is decorated so fine,
That satan uses as a lure?
What ornament does he dangle,
To make your mind, impure?
Oh how we need You, Lord,
For we can be, tantalized.

48

Many things that tantalize us are not as harmless as the ornaments, that capture our kitty's attention. And if we are to keep our minds clean, our hearts pure in our world today—we must stay close in fellowship with the Lord. So many things can lure us and keep us from keeping God as our first priority. And not all of them are even bad pursuits. It is not always direct sin that gets us chasing headlong down a wrong path.

Sometimes busyness, not having safeguards in place—in our relationships, or accountability in our friendships, etc.—can trigger us to be led astray. Not to mention outright disobedience, what we do or where we go, or how we put ourselves in situations that we know may make us vulnerable to trouble spots. These less obvious "gray areas" can be as dangerous as those things that we know are wrong in our hearts.

If we want to be kept safely under the everlasting arms of God's grace, we must ask the Lord to direct us, to give us discernment. We must give Him time, our devotion, and love. For only in keeping our attention fixed upon the Savior, can we tune-out the distractions that are ever dangling before each of us.

Satan knows our weaknesses; but God is stronger, He is our Defender. Call upon the name of the Lord and He will be your Warrior. Even Jesus was tempted by Satan, but He did not sin! One decision, or one prayer—determines—which way we will go. But either choice may have lasting consequences.

....

....

Tiger Lily was a good girl; she did not even bat the "pretties." It was a sign that she was growing and learning. That is a sign of maturity on our part too. That is when God looks at us and says, "they are my Disciples." "They are learning my lessons, following my heart." Surely the space of His heart swells with pride, just as mine did, when my baby did not heed to her natural inclination. She did not give in to temptation's pull. She just enjoyed the lights and the joy of the season.

There are things that will be so … tempting; that is why we need the strength of the Lord to teach us to walk in His ways. One right choice at a time, will bring us closer to walking with our Lord. As we mature in our faith, He will be a light in the darkness, helping us not to succumb to temptation.

....

....

Her eyes are alight with wonder,
Her paws activate with play.
'Tis the merriest of seasons,
Excitement, changes with each day.
She's the very picture,
Of joy that cannot be contained.
She runs, she dances,
Until, only breeze, remains.
And though she "bats" the decorations,
I wait for the moments when she is still …
As she curls-up in a ball,
She takes a catnap to rest, until …
Her eyes alight with wonder,
Her paws activate with play.
'Tis the merriest of seasons,
Somehow she senses the coming,
Of Christmas Day!

Does the spirit of Christmas fill your heart with joy—that cannot be contained? If we are Christ-followers, this should be our state-of-being, everyday. We should have a contagious energy and hope about us—even in the midst of struggle. We should stand-out in the midst of trials, knowing that our help, comes from Almighty God.

"When the angels had gone away from them into heaven, the shepherds began saying to one another, 'Let us go straight to Bethlehem then, and see this thing that has happened which the Lord has made known to us.' So they came in a hurry and found their way to Mary and Joseph, and the baby as He lay in the manger. When they had seen this, they made known the statement which had been told them about this Child. And all who heard it wondered at the things which were told them by the shepherds. But Mary treasured all these things, pondering them in her heart."
Luke 2:15-19 NASB

Joy should not waver. It means having a sense of peace and trust in the Lord when things are not going the way we want. It is believing that He will walk with us—through—the hits. Resting in Him builds our faith. It creates a deeper spirit of thankfulness for His faithfulness. It's deciding to trust and dwell on God's grace and faithful care of us—not on the thing—happening to us, even when it's something we would not have chosen.

The decorations, the lights, the glow, the excitement of Christmas— are not meant for only a season—they are one of the building blocks of faith—joy. If yours is contained, ask God to activate it. Rest, then run, into the merriest, abundant life, that He has in store. This does not mean that nothing will ever be shattered or broken—but that the Lord will be with you, to fill you with Himself, His strength, and surround you with His love.

Joy, that cannot be contained, is contagious. It will draw others to you, and thus to Christ, Who lives in your heart. But don't keep Him only for Christmas day! Be filled with wonder. Activate. Anticipate. Share your spunk and His Spirit, everywhere you go. Keep a spirit of ponder, ever alive in your heart. This is how we maintain joy!

"For the Lord your God is living among you. He is a mighty savior. He will take delight in you with gladness. With his love, he will calm all your fears. He will rejoice over you with joyful songs." Zephaniah 3:17 NLT

Leaving a Paw Print
>   Psalm 16:11, 1 Peter 1:8-9, John 15:11, Psalm 9:2,
>   3 John 1:4, Psalm 19:8

Room to pause in the Paw Print

....

....

....

....

Snow, like Feathers

The snow looked like downy-feathers,
As it fluttered to the ground.
It seemed to whisper this morning,
Of God's glory,
Without making a sound.
Each lofty snowflake reminded me,
Of cotton attached to invisible thread.
Lace, seemed to be woven from heaven,
And fell gently on my face and head.
Tiger Lily adores it,
Her purr goes on and on.
It looked like a decoration of the season,
Cheer that's here,
And then, too soon, is gone.
She sat at the window,
From the time the first flakes fell.
She chattered at the birds in flight,
With an amazing story, she had to tell;
It was as if she wanted to be included,
In singing a song unto the Lord.
As each angel-wing hit her,
It seemed joy, from her heart poured.
It was just one more example,
Of how God's presence,
Touches our lives with grace.
For this softest brush of His goodness,
Gives us, one more glimpse,
Of His omnipotent face.

Each of our cats has liked the snow; but Tiger Lily, loves it. She is drawn to it from her first glimpse of the flakes, until a fresh bowl is delivered to her tastebuds. She loves to hear the birds singing and watches them through its falling. In fact, she joins them with her little chatter. She can't wait to dip her paws into its downy softness. And if a cat could sigh in delight, she most certainly would.

I often look at creation and think … that is why God created certain birds, animals, or things, just like snow; I think He wants to delight us. I think He wants to be revered as Father and King of Kings, but I think He also wants to see us smile, and hear us laugh. I hope in every day, you find something of His goodness, some soft brush of His presence. It is before you, right in front of your eyes. But you can't get too busy, or you may miss things—like *the snow like feathers*—that can fall upon you.

If you look for the hand of the Lord, He will show Himself, and He will always give you a reason to find joy in any day. You may even find yourself "purring," or singing a song of praise. That's when you'll know you are in tune with His Spirit and walking in His grace. Snow like feathers, may be just the beginning … of you learning to hear His voice in the call of nature. It's the stirring you feel within your soul.

Leaving a Paw Print
Isaiah 55:10-11, Psalm 148:7-9

Take Delight in All His Gifts

As I held Tilly in my arms,
The falling snow held her attention.
It brought her unrestrained wonder.
She brought me delight,
At her amazement,
Her curiosity,
At her complete joy,
In this single moment.

"Delight yourself in Adonai, and he will give you the requests of your heart."
Psalm 37:4 TLV

Do you have a sense of wonder,
Toward the God,
Who creates the falling snow?
Did you ever catch a feathered-flake,
As its beauty flutters,
To the ground, here, below?
Do you appreciate these moments,
Of perfect joy?

Does your heart,
Ever simply overflow with thanksgiving?
Do you ever just look-up,
And give God your adoring praise?
Have you ever just spun,
Like a child,
In a circle,
With your arms or heart, purely raised?

Delighting ourselves in the Lord, means that He is our focus. From the first moment that we wake, to the hour that we lay our head on the pillow at night, it means that we seek Him. And I believe that He has given us so much—that every day of our lives—should be filled with a little worship.

Delight by definition means to have joy. It's a feeling of enjoyment or to take pleasure in something. The Lord delights in caring for us, and delivering beauty into our lives, like snow. Yet some miss this simple miracle. They see it as a nuisance or a burden. If you will trust that whatever God allows to fall in your life—has a purpose—you will soon learn to see your circumstances through His perspective.

Delight is evident when you look at Tilly. It is evident in my eyes as well. Do you know that this is how Jesus is looking at you? He loves you like this! He wants to hold you close, and wants you to discover that everything that touches your life—has value, or a purpose, or will bring about beauty. If not at the moment, it will unfold like your faith.

"For to us a child is born, to us a son is given, and the government will be on his shoulders. And he will be called Wonderful Counselor, Mighty God, Everlasting Father, Prince of Peace." Isaiah 9:6 NIV

Raise your eyes, raise your arms, raise your praise. Take delight in the Savior—and all of His creations, and soon you may just find that you cannot contain—your joy. Take delight in all of God's gifts—especially His love for you. For when you absorb this truth, you will see Him purely, like freshly falling snow.

Look to Him for all your needs—as the Son, Your Wonderful Counselor, Mighty God, Everlasting Father, and Prince of Peace. For when you embrace Him in each of these facets, you will find delight and joy in serving and loving the One true God, Who loves you with fullest, complete, unabashed joy!

How do you take delight in His gifts?

....

....

Life is a Gift

Do you remember a certain gift that you got for Christmas or some other special occasion? Can you recall a few special things that brought your heart delight? Perhaps it was something that you had your eye on for quite some time? Or maybe it was something that you desperately needed? Maybe it was from your spouse, and it was a splurge? Or it was a surprise from an unexpected source, like a "secret sister?"

As I would wrap presents for Doug, or for our family members back East when we lived away from home, I almost always had a companion. Jeepers (and each of our cats at the time) would come to assist me. They, of course, would want to lie on the tissue, or tug on the ribbons, or sit on the wrapping paper. They always showed up to participate.

We may not always remember an exact gift. In fact as we age, we tend to remember events, things that we do—where we've lived, visited, those we have done life with—over objects. You cherish your family, your friends, and the love and affection that you've shared—even with your pets. These are the things that give you perspective.

Each day is the gift.
This life, this time.
Right now,
This moment …

… What we do with it,
With whom we choose to share,
Are the presents for our memory,
The ways we show we care.

These, are the treasures,
That we want to accumulate.
These are the things, precious,
That we want to articulate.

For life is short …
It moves swiftly by.
Oh Jesus draw us closer,
Till we reach,
The great by and by.

Life, is the gift. And God has a package, all wrapped and tied with a bow—it's His perfect Will that's been specifically designed for us. But we must open our hearts and our hands—with trust, with humility. We must come like a child to receive the gifts of His grace, love, and mercy. 'Cause this is a gift you'll remember. It is an experience that will surprise and delight you. It will be a treasure for today and will bring an eternal promise. And you will want to share the contents of your discovery!

A life surrendered to Jesus is like a gift to be opened, one day at a time. Love, faithfulness and grace, teach us to trust the One Who is our guide. He draws us by His loving-kindness, into His presence. He offers us moment-by-moment strength and hope and peace. Have you chosen to accept the gift of life?

Leaving a Paw Print
Lamentations 3:22-23, John 3:16-17, Acts 2:38, 2 Corinthians 9:15, Ephesians 2:8-9, James 1:17

Room to pause in the Paw Print

The Babe in Her Arms

I take such delight in those times that I am able to hold Tiger Lily. Due to a few "tummy" issues, she can be a bit fussy when we pick her up or cuddle her too snuggly. We give her special food, and she requires a little TLC, to alleviate these symptoms.

In addition, we allow her to come to us for affection, to sit beside us, and we brush her gently (for as long as she will allow). We cherish moments like this (on the stairs), or when we travel, or take her to the Vet—when she invites a little more closeness.

And as much as we have loved each of our cats, I can only imagine the joy that Mary must have felt when she held baby Jesus in her arms for the first time. I wonder if all of the events of the preceding months flashed before her eyes. I wonder if she was so filled with love, that her newborn—the very Savior of the World—would be swaddled in cloths and was tucked-in, near her heart.

I imagine that most of you have had some measure of this feeling. Whether you have tenderly held your own child, a family or friend's baby, or a beloved furry companion ... you probably have experienced the miracle, that is birth. And when it is the one that you have given birth to, or chosen to be part of your family—you feel love—that has no equal.

That is the kind of love that Jesus came so humbly to bring into the world. This Babe, born of a virgin, arrived, not with fanfare, but into a quiet little village. He was born near an inn where there was no room for Him and his parents. He was surrounded by Mary and Joseph, shepherds, and those who sought to know the Messiah. Yet His life would change history. His grace will wrap around every heart that willingly seeks His mercy. His hope fills every soul that makes room for Him as Savior (Luke 1 & 2).

I can't know if you will have many or few gathered around you this Christmas. I don't know if many or few arms, will embrace you in this holy season. But I can tell you this ... the One Who was born in the manger would become a perfect, sinless, man. He would die at age 33, upon the Cross, to give you life. His arms were stretched out in an embrace. His eyes are filled with love and light. He is seeking those who will come like a child, to receive His gift of grace.

Take one step, make room. He loves you with an ever-lasting love, and wants to give you an ever-lasting hope, joy, and eternity in His presence. Come get your hug, get adopted. Come, walk with the One Who knows your name and everything about you. Jesus, is, was, and will always be—the One Who loves you perfectly. Will you humbly open your heart to let Him be Your Master and Friend?

Leaving a Paw Print
John 3:16-17, Ephesians 1:5, James 4:8, Revelation 3:20

One of my best friends sent Tiger Lily a gift card for Christmas. So I sent her this picture of us from her completed "shopping spree." I loved that we were able to capture T.L.'s face … as if she thought … "Is this all for me?"

Have you ever looked at your life like this? Have you ever felt—even with difficulty, concerns, everything that may not be going right, … perhaps while enduring some illness or pain— that still, you have so much to be grateful for?

God, sometimes I think,
"Is this all for me?
Did you give your Son,
So that I could be free?
I find myself grateful,
Blessed indeed,
To know that Your grace and love,
Give me all that I need … to believe."

The Lord provides for our needs, and if we find ourselves with a few treats along the way, it is good to show our appreciation and gratitude. For if His Spirit is alive in us, we are indeed blessed—rich —in the things that really matter. When we learn to trust Him and appreciate the small things, He often entrusts us with gifts to be shared.

If we view what we have in this light, we will be content. It is in *wanting more* that we can think that God is not enough. He is the One Who can give us—everything. He already did, Jesus. And yes, He did it all—for you (and for me).

"Is this all for me?", is an attitude that helps us appreciate what we have and keeps our focus on how God is providing for us. Everything—comes from His gracious hand.

"Thanks be to God for his inexpressible gift!" 2 Corinthians 9:15 ESV

"On coming to the house, they saw the child with his mother Mary, and they bowed down and worshiped him. Then they opened their treasures and presented him with gifts of gold, frankincense and myrrh."
Matthew 2:10-11 NIV

Magi, wisemen from the East, came to Jerusalem. They had followed a singular star, seeking a singular Babe. They came to bring gifts and their adoration to this holy infant.

As I was thinking of this scene, I was reminded of this little pillow. It was a gift from my brother and sister-in-love from a Christmas-past. And I began to imagine … if these kitties could offer us gifts of the season … what might they suggest? With their eyes focused upward toward heaven, I thought of these: paws (a pause), a purr (a merry spirit) and praise (humble adoration) unto the baby Jesus, but also unto Him as the King of Kings.

It's the Holy season,
It's the hectic season;
It's the time of year,
When we run around,
Buying, giving, baking, serving—
Enjoying, every sight and sound.

…But as I begin to ponder,
Amidst my Christmas list,
Preparing my cards and greetings,
Jesus, showed me a few things, I missed …

… Upon a little pillow,
There were three wise-cats.

Upon their faces,
Was the expression—wonder;
Would you look at that?!
    Jesus, seemed to draw my eyes,
    Making it crystal clear,
    That there were three things,
    That He asked of me,
    But first, I had to draw near.
        Come and bring your pause,
        Stop, make room for a little stillness.
        Purr, come speak what's in your heart.
            Praise, don't forget your adoration,
            For Christmas, is, after all,
            His Birthday;
            He came with love, to impart.

It's easy to get so busy that we don't take time to give the Lord any reverence, any stillness, any praise. And yet, these are the things that we need, in order to love Him and others, and to complete our lists. If we want to have the mind and heart of Christ in this season, we need to make Him a priority.

Bring your paws—humbly, tell the Lord that you are willing to do as He directs—to love Him and others, in this Holy season. Create a little stillness, time to reflect, to energize your mind and body, for this pleases our Lord.

Bring a purr—a merry spirit to all that you do. Pray and ask for strength, wisdom and guidance, in how to give to those who need some care, love and encouragement.

Bring your praise—give Jesus—your humble attention, your heartfelt adoration.

When Jesus holds first place in our lives—our paws, purrs, and praise—will reflect His heart of love.

Leaving a Paw Print
Psalm 46:10, Psalm 100, Philippians 2:9-11

Room to pause in the Paw Print

....

....

....

....

Surprise

It appeared that we caught Tilly in a look of surprise as she had jumped into the midst of the gift preparations. Her eyes were huge, as if she had been caught peeking into the gift within. Did you ever do that as a kid? Ever shake the packages to see what was inside? Did you wake up early on Christmas morning because you couldn't wait to investigate your new toys and presents?

I love how each of the characters of the Biblical account were met with a sense of awe, of surprise, as miraculous events happened to each—in the unfolding of the ultimate miracle—Jesus' birth.

There were angels—from single sightings, to hosts of them gathered in the heavenly realms. There were songs of praise. There were assurances given to calm fears. There were gifts given. There were shepherds and wisemen drawn to the manger scene via a star. There was divine protection given to Mary and Joseph from a king who sought to kill them. And there was the holy presence of Father God, ushering His beloved Son to earth, as His gift to all mankind.

What was your sweetest surprise as a child? How about as an adult? If you were one of the Biblical characters from the Luke 2 account—what would most fill you with adoration?

....

....

....

Take a few minutes to meditate with the Lord, and let Him usher in ... a sense of beholding. For the One Who came so long ago ... will one day return ... as a surprise, to call His children to His side. That fills me with wonder and praise. It keeps me thankful for His gift of Salvation, everyday.

Do you see what I see?
A kitty's face hides within the snowy mountain chain.
He's seeking a bird,
That flies upon the plains!

I love being observant to what my cat sees. I often bow to his/her level to get a cat's-eye view of life. It's an interesting perspective, since they are a little shorter than we. Maybe that's why it's a constant struggle to keep them off counters and high places. They are in search of a higher perspective!

I couldn't resist testing your "I spy" skills in this photo. Did you find both the cat and the bird? Did you know that Jesus is not hiding from you, but instead wants you to seek to know Him, and have a personal relationship with Him?

I think the wonders of creation are one of the ways that He is constantly reaching out to us. I think He gives us extraordinary glimpses of Himself in our ordinary days. But we must be looking for a higher perspective—on our lives, in our circumstances.

Do you think the Lord ever wants to ask us: Do you see what I see? Do you try to understand My love, My grace, My forgiveness? Are you still long enough to absorb My Word and its truths? Do you listen when you pray or simply pour out your requests and walk away?

This might be a good place for each of us to pause and do a simple heart check. Did any of those questions, resonate? Give the Lord room to answer.

....

....

....

Do you see the Christ-Child,
In the manger where He lay?
Will you invite Him into your heart,
Or leave Him swaddled,
In the cradle's hay?

Do you see ... that God invites each of us to know Him—in interesting, subtle, bold, extraordinary and ordinary—ways? But we must be attuned to discover the many facets of His character, the breadth and width of His love, and the depth of His mercy. For when we seek, He promises, that we'll find!

Leaving a Paw Print
> Romans 1:20, 1 Timothy 2:1-6, Isaiah 55:8-9,
> Psalm 103, Matthew 7:7-8

Room to pause in the Paw Print

....

....

Two of my Favorite Things

> I held two of my favorite things,
> Right here in my arms—
> Chocolate,
> And my Tiger Lily.
> Now obviously,
> I cannot share,
> This sweet treat,
> With our precious feline.
> But the comparison,
> Is useful,
> Because we all find,
> A few earthly things ...
> To be simply, divine.

What are a few of your favorite things? Would your feline or chocolate appear on your list? I know my dear-boy-hubby, would be at the top of mine, along with coffee, tea, flowers, and spending time with Jesus, as well as enjoying anything of His creation (in no particular order!) Does a certain trip, a specific food, or your kids—come to the fore of your thoughts? What about a certain memory?

When I was a young child, my dad brought home a 25 pound Hershey bar for our entire family. It made for one sweet and delightful Christmas for all of us. And since Doug knew that was a tender remembrance, he was excited to find a 10 pound version one year. We were both delighted when Tilly hopped up into my arms. She wanted to investigate, not only her Christmas goodies, but ours as well.

Did you know that Jesus takes great delight in you, as His creation? As His child? Did you know that He loves to meet not only your needs, but also to provide you with surprises and treats? He adores bringing delight to our hearts—not just in the holiday season—but every day.

Another of my favorite things? To look for the evidence of His care and faithfulness. In fact, I like to keep a little journal of how Jesus is answering prayer, or how He is shaping events in my life.

I also like to ask friends and family to share at least 3 things that they are grateful for. This encourages not only my heart, but their own—to see how wonderfully the Lord provides for each of us. It also helps us realize that He is with us in times of difficulty, sorrow, or when we are experiencing our highest levels of achievement or joy. This brings delight to my heart—I hope it does to yours, also.

Leaving a Paw Print

> Psalm 149:4, Psalm 117:2, Psalm 22:8, Psalm 147:11, Jeremiah 9:24, Lamentations 3:22-23 & 25, Psalm 36:5

Room to pause in the Paw Print

....

....

....

A Purr of Prayer

Dear Lord, for my husband, for our feline, for Your very love and presence, and every good gift that You bestow—I am forever grateful. I am so appreciative of everything that You do for me. I give You praise, in order to give You glory. Please accept my worship like a hug. It is my affection, to show my delight in You. Amen.

Is one of your favorite things to show Jesus your appreciation and give Him your love?

She's a Good Girl

She's a good girl,
Please feed her promptly.
She's a good girl,
It's time for her favorite toy.
She's a good girl,
She'll take a little hug now.
She's a good girl,
Well maybe, *not,* right now!
She's a good girl,
As long as she gets her way.

She's a good girl,
Just don't try to move her.
She's a good girl,
Just don't touch her tummy.
She's a good girl.
Just don't change her routine.
She's a good girl,
Almost ... nearly ... always.
Is she really any different,
From, you and me?

Tiger Lily wasn't such a good-girl the day she began climbing the Christmas tree. She was all paws-and-excitement—as this was the first one that she had ever seen. She was only 8-months-old in this photo, so this was also her first time experiencing all the delights of the holiday season and the variety of my decorations. What was interesting is, that she was a good-girl after all the "pretties" had been added. Then, for the most part, she just sat and gazed ... but her behavior definitely depended on the time or the moment.

Do you see any similarity between the feline and us? If Jesus were to evaluate us ... would He say, "Yes, my child is a good girl (or guy), when everything in their life goes smoothly?" But if He asks us—to change jobs, or routines, or requires us to move—would the answer be the same? Are we passive, or aggressive, or accepting—when something interrupts our "blessed" life?

Is our attitude, based only on what God is doing for us—keeping us happy—rather than upon our love for Him? Is there a steady, flowing trust between us? Do we act up, if we don't get our way, or our prayers aren't answered, just so? Do we hiss or claw or scratch—against God's Will—or lash out at others, when God allows a little wilderness-trek or a mountainous climb?

Tiger Lily is a good girl most of the time. She is sweet and affectionate. But naturally, we do all we can to keep her happy and well cared for. We know when she likes to be fed, how she likes to be petted, and how to help her adapt when our routines must change, or we have to move.

Cats, like people, are adaptable. But as I was thinking about what she likes/dislikes and how her behavior coincides with whether her world remains stable, it gave me pause. Do we have a similar expectation of the Lord? Are we happy, when all is good? Angry/reactive, if illness, doubt and fear, come pawing at us?

....

Because we serve a good God, His Spirit continually works within us, to work all things for good—to those who love Him and obey His Will (Romans 8:28)—even those things that we don't understand.

Lord, may we be a "good girl" or "good guy" in your eyes, always. May we trust You with the changes, with the challenges, with everything that You allow to touch us. For if our attitudes are controlled by Your Spirit, we will maintain a sense of peace and joy —no matter what our routine, or what any given day holds. Because when we believe that we are held in the Master's care, we know that You are good—and that You are always with us! Amen.

Room for your Purr of Prayer

....

....

....

We will never be "good" on our own. We all sin and fall short of the glory of God. Only Jesus is perfect. But if we are surrendered as His child—He wraps us in love, grace, mercy and forgiveness. Our good, good Lord, clothes us in His righteousness, when we pause and praise, and acknowledge that we need Him, daily.

What is Christmas?

What does the word "Christmas" conjure in your mind? Like the cat, do you jump "all-in" to see what it holds? Do you associate this season with a sense of joy in your heart or face it with dread?

Perhaps you are blessed with idyllic memories of December? Possibly you had a wonderful day … but an awful Christmas night? Or maybe there are leftover unhealthy messages from childhood? Or currently, are there difficult relationships you must navigate? Trust me, you are not alone.

Do you know that Mary and Joseph, the main characters of the Biblical account of Jesus' birth, did not have an easy first Christmas? Here they were, engaged, promised to one another. They both received an angelic visitation, announcing the impossible surprise: they would have a son—a holy, perfect child—not through human conception, but through the Holy Spirit.

Imagine, the scorn they endured! Imagine how they must have felt— like the Lord was leading them—out on a limb—of courage, of faith. So does the Lord understand pain filled memories? You bet! Does He help us deal with loss, or the remnants of it—year after year? Again, a resounding yes!

The Babe of the Manger grew to be the Son of Man. He is still perfect. He is the One Who guides us, teaches us, and leads us to praise Him. He can help us control our reactions (our hiss), and help us love, purely, wholly, like He does. He covers us with grace. So no matter where you are geographically, emotionally or spiritually this Christmas—I implore you—to run, jump, leap—into the arms of Jesus. Look up, into the eyes that adore you. Hold fast to the One Who can lead you into eternal life. For that is the greatest gift that He can give you, or you can give yourself in this beautiful time of year.

A Purr of Prayer

Dear Lord, may You touch every heart with a sense of Your nearness in some new and unique way. May we see Your light and feel Your love, like an embrace that holds us tenderly and does not let go. For this is why You came into the world. It is how You enter every heart that seeks You like a child. Fill us with the wonder of Who You are, Jesus, as we celebrate this lovely season with our families, friends, and our felines. And may we rest in Your care, knowing that nothing will ever surprise You about our lives, about our journey. In You we trust … today, into the New Year … and into eternity. Amen.

Leaving a Paw Print

> Matthew 1:18-25, Luke 1:14, Luke 2:11, 1 John 4:7,10 &16,
> Romans 5:5, Psalm 107:1, 1 Peter 5:6-7

Room to pause in the Paw Print

....

....

What is Christmas? It's a time to see Jesus as the Babe, the Son, the Morning Star, the Risen Christ, and the Messiah. Christmas is the most wonderful time of the year to call Him, Lord and Master.

What's in a Name?

Remember the time you took to name your child? How about the special thought you gave in naming your furry companion? And don't you love to hear the sound of your name on the lips of loved ones? Well, cats are no different.

Tiger Lilly—loves to be called—to playtime, to dinner time, to simply join us as we work. She comes running when we return from errands, or when we are ready to turn-in for the night. She responds to her name, because it means that she is loved, she belongs.

Names, hold meaning. How they are spoken, enunciated, can convey many emotions to us. And names themselves, have definitions. Take the name of Jesus, Immanuel, for instance; it means, "God with us."

Isaiah 9:6 (NKJV) gives us some descriptive language, some adjectives, that proclaim Him to be holy, righteous, sovereign and just. Let's take a look at this text: *"For unto us a Child is born, unto us a Son is given; and the government will be upon His shoulder. And His name will be called Wonderful, Counselor, Mighty God, Everlasting Father, Prince of Peace."*

In any situation, these names are powerful in finding God to be faithful. But they also show us that He is near.

Exercise: Take each name, each descriptive word, and think of a time that the Lord displayed Himself to you in this way. Then thank Him, for this is how we discover that He is personal to us and that we are loved and belong to Him. Call out to Jesus, today!

Tilly loves to come sit closely beside me as I have my quiet time with the Lord. In this photo, you can see just how close—within about 6 inches. She's intimately connected to me as her momma', care taker and guardian, because we've developed a bond of trust that's implicit.

Jesus wants to have a personal relationship with you. His invitation was written to your heart in the way He came to earth, so gently. It was lived out in the example of His time spent serving the Father, and in the way He ministered to the hearts of His disciples and mankind. And it was displayed as love and mercy upon the Cross of Calvary.

Here's your turn to draw close
Dear Jesus, I see my need of You as Companion and Savior. I come, confessing and acknowledging my sinful nature and ask You to be my Good Shepherd, the Lord of my life. Forgive me. Save me; and let Your Spirit be the Guide of my steps. I'm drawing close, Master, and ask You to do the same as I become part of Your family. Amen.

If you've already been adopted
Dear Jesus, I come, especially in this Christmas season with a renewed commitment to cherish the gift of my Salvation, Your grace, and love. Grant me the courage to share this gift, not only with those who are closest to me, but with my co-workers, friends, and neighbors. And Lord, help me to grow in the grace and knowledge of Who You are, so that I mature—in faith, in trust, in my following of You, I pray. Amen.

Tilly's coming close reminds me of our bond of love. It's how I show my devotion to Jesus as well. It's how He demonstrates to my heart that He is with me—as I read His Word, pray and follow His Will. Will you come close to let God show you how dear you are to Him?

Prayer of my Heart

To my Best Friend, Jesus, I love this holy season; I cherish this time of year that is set apart to honor Your birth, when the lights come out, and the spirit of kindness and joy seems to permeate the very atmosphere. I love all the preparations, the writing of Christmas cards, decking the halls, the tree, etc. But most of all, I love the quiet moments when it's our simple family—my hubby and I, and our kitty—enjoying a night at home.

For it's in these gentle times, that I feel Your Spirit most nearly and hear Your voice whisper to my soul—that You came as a Babe—so that all could identify with Who You are. You've walked on earth; You know its joys, its challenges, its struggles and heartaches. And in Your humility, You became the gift of the Cross via the manger.

Thank You, Jesus, for love that was displayed in every step of Your life. Thank You for Your sacrificial and gracious example. May all that I do, give, and share, be done with the motivation and from the source of Your strength, I pray. Amen.

Your moment to pause

How does knowing Jesus *(or not)* affect your view of the Christmas season? How does it change how you give, work, and share with those around you?

....

....

....

Your turn to talk to God

Dear Jesus, help me to see more of You this year. Focus my eyes, not on the external blessings of Christmas, the ...

....

that usually catches my eye, or creates busyness in my schedule, but instead, to allow You to work within my heart in this area:

.... Amen.

The decorations were up,
Scents of Christmas filled the air.
Muffin, enjoyed the sights and sounds,
In this blessed season that's bright and fair.
He drew near the fireplace,
Where warmth seeped into the room.
The countdown to Christmas Eve,
Very nearly, loomed.

The carols began to echo. The lights were all a-glitter. The tree and house had gotten decked-out to purely shine. There's a little more kindness in the air. And the celebration of Jesus' birth draws our hearts closer to one another. Friends and families, near and far, make plans to gather. All of these things combine—to make this sacred day, special, to one and all.

Every eye is alight with a special glow. Love comes near to all creation and humankind. The Baby, born in Bethlehem so long ago, *is* the gift. He is the warmth. He is the star of this Holy Night. Are you drawing near, to behold the true gift of the season?

Jesus came to be our warmth, our peace. He is the One, Who fills us with wonder. Let us behold Him with awe, far above all that glitters and shines on earth. For His glory, radiates beyond this day into the Universe, into eternity, into the heart of every soul that believes upon His holy name.

I went outside to take a picture of our Christmas lights ... and as I looked up ... there sat Tiger Lily at the front door. She made me smile, and made me think of the verses in John 14:1-3, where Jesus tells us that "He is preparing a place for us" ... and that "where He is, we may be also." Since our cat is a little like my shadow, it got me to thinking ... that I want to be Jesus' shadow. I want to be where He is, not just in heaven (our future home), but here and now, on earth.

As the lights of Christmas glow from houses, store windows, churches, and illuminate towns all around the world, I pray that God's presence is like a shadow, wrapping you with love. I wish for you to know His delight when you seek His company. And I hope all the stars help you look up, to see the Savior. For this is the season to see Him and feel joy, or comfort, or peace, or goodwill. (Or whatever you need, right now!)

The Father is definitely preparing a place for those who love Him, but our place, while we are here, is to share His love and light—right on our own street, in our own community, in our own homes. For light dispels the shadows, and love transforms every heart that it touches.

Leaving a Paw Print Ephesians 5:1, 1 Peter 2:9, & 21

Inspiration, came from Tiger Lily, sitting in her carpeted perch. Her multi-level retreat sits in the corner between two windows. As she was softly nestled in its curve, it appeared that she waited patiently for me to draw back the curtains to let in the light. As I kissed the top of her head to give her a little love, these words began forming in my mind …

Let in some light,
Let in some love,
Let in His spirit,
That flows from, above.

Let in some hope,
Let in some grace,
Let in some worship,
Of God's majestic face.

Let in some peace,
Let in some joy,
Let it light up the countenance,
Of every man, woman, girl and boy.

For when you let in all of these things, you give Jesus room to let His love shine through you. And that is the plan and the purpose, of Christmas.

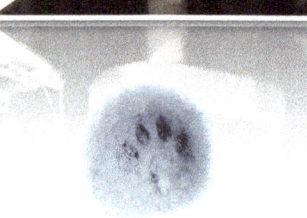

Let in the light,
Let in the love.
Let in the miracle of the season,
Radiate, wonder that comes from above …
To shine, forevermore.

A Purr of Prayer

Dear Jesus, please teach my heart to let in Your love and light every day, so that it saturates my soul and becomes a beacon to reflect Who You are to the world. Amen.

Room for your Purr of Prayer

....

....

"For God, who said, 'Let there be light in the darkness,' has made this light shine in our hearts so we could know the glory of God that is seen in the face of Jesus Christ." 2 Corinthians 4:6 NLT

We came across this kitty while we were out walking one day; or I should say, she found us. In fact, her melodious meows reached us

before we could see her. She followed us for some distance, singing her little heart out. We engaged with her, stopped and petted her, and she purred and continued to give us her sweet greetings.

Well, now that you've read about the account of Jesus birth, (perhaps for the first time, or with a fresh perspective), you've got some Good News to share! Christmas is a great time —to sing of God's faithfulness. It provides a wonderful opportunity to invite friends and family to a candle-light or other service at your church. And it's a special time to meet a need or encourage someone who is hurting—to demonstrate the love of Jesus.

I love that the Luke 2 account of Jesus' birth is filled with greetings— angelic ones that brought prophetic tidings of things that would occur, the blessed words "do not fear," and a host of angels who ushered in praise to give God glory. There were even greetings of God's creatures, as the animals of the inn surrounded the manger scene.

So what's your greeting? Along with Merry Christmas, or whichever phrase you use ... how will you sing-out the message of this Holy season? For just like our kitty above, God is praised when anything/ anyone of His creatures/creations shows its adoration and tells of His goodness and grace.

"And he said to them, 'Go into all the world and proclaim the gospel to the whole creation.'" Mark 16:15 ESV

Leaving a Paw Print

Luke 2:10, Revelation 14:6, Psalm 96:3, 1 Chronicles 16:8, Psalm 67:1-3, Psalm 66:1-2

Sing-out with the Good News of Jesus' birth, His love and His mission of grace. For in the telling, you may find a little joy fills not only your heart, but brings joy to the world.

Spend some time in Companionship with the Lord

Isaiah 9:6 (NIV) "For to us a child is born, to us a son is given, and the government will be on his shoulders. And he will be called Wonderful Counselor, Mighty God, Everlasting Father, Prince of Peace."

Isaiah 7:14 (AMP) "Therefore the Lord Himself will give you a sign: Listen carefully, the virgin will conceive and give birth to a son, and she will call his name Immanuel (God with us)."

Luke 1:14 (GW) "He will be your pride and joy, and many people will be glad that he was born."

Luke 1:35 (HCSB) "The angel replied to her: 'The Holy Spirit will come upon you, and the power of the Most High will overshadow you. Therefore, the holy One to be born will be called the Son of God.'"

Luke 1:38 (VOICE) "Here I am, the Lord's humble servant. As you have said, let it be done to me. And the heavenly messenger was gone."

Luke 2:4-6 (ESV) "And Joseph also went up from Galilee, from the town of Nazareth, to Judea, to the city of David, which is called Bethlehem, because he was of the house and lineage of David, to be registered with Mary, his betrothed, who was with child. And while they were there, the time came for her to give birth."

Luke 2:7 (NKJV) "And she brought forth her firstborn Son, and wrapped Him in swaddling cloths, and laid Him in a manger, because there was no room for them in the inn."

Luke 2:40 (GW) "The child grew and became strong. He was filled with wisdom, and God's favor was with him."

Luke 2:51 (GNT) "So Jesus went back with them to Nazareth, where he was obedient to them. His mother treasured all these things in her heart."

Matthew 2:10 (TLV) "When they saw the star, they rejoiced exceedingly with great gladness."

John 1:14 (ICB) "The Word became a man and lived among us. We saw his glory—the glory that belongs to the only Son of the Father. The Word was full of grace and truth."

Philippians 2:7 (EXB) "But he gave up his place with God and made himself nothing [emptied himself]. He became like [took the form of] a servant [slave; bondservant] and was born as a man [in the likeness of humanity/ men]."

John 3:16 (GW) "God loved the world this way: He gave his only Son so that everyone who believes in him will not die but will have eternal life."

John 14:6 (NASB) "Jesus said to him, 'I am the way, and the truth, and the life; no one comes to the Father but through Me.'"

Romans 5:1-2 (ERV) "We have been made right with God because of our faith. So we have peace with God through our Lord Jesus Christ. Through our faith, Christ has brought us into that blessing of God's grace that we now enjoy. And we are very happy because of the hope we have of sharing God's glory."

Revelation 22:16 (NIV) "I, Jesus, have sent my angel to give you this testimony for the churches. I am the Root and the Offspring of David, and the bright Morning Star."

John 8:12 (NKJV) "Then Jesus spoke to them again, saying, 'I am the light of the world. He who follows Me shall not walk in darkness, but have the light of life.'"

John 1:4 (HCSB) "Life was in Him, and that life was the light of men."

John 1:29 (NIV) "The next day John saw Jesus coming toward him and said, 'Look, the Lamb of God, who takes away the sin of the world!'"

2 Corinthians 4:6 (GNT) "The God who said, 'Out of darkness the light shall shine!' is the same God who made his light shine in our hearts, to bring us the knowledge of God's glory shining in the face of Christ."

Psalm 43:3 (ASV) "Oh send out thy light and thy truth; let them lead me: let them bring me unto thy holy hill, and to thy tabernacles."

Ephesians 1:18 (NASB) "I pray that the eyes of your heart may be enlightened, so that you will know what is the hope of His calling, what are the riches of the glory of His inheritance in the saints ..."

Revelation 17:14 (VOICE) "Together they will make war on the Lamb, and the Lamb will be victorious over them because He is the Lord over all lords and the King over all kings; and those who stand with Him are called, elect, and faithful."

Happy, Meowy Christmas Summary

A little china cat-set in the oriental market caught my eye. With the words, Happy Christmas, my mind conjured images of how each of our cats have seemed to sense and anticipate the opening of the containers as I begin to decorate for the holiday season. Their eyes seem to glow and sparkle like a child's. The very air appears to come alive and their little furry bodies are filled with joy as if they too, know something big is about to take place.

As we celebrate the birth of the Christ-Child, Jesus, we also pause to adore Him—as Wonderful Counselor, Mighty God, Everlasting Father, and Prince of Peace (Isaiah 9:6).

From the star that shone above Bethlehem, to the canopy that adorns the nightly sky, we are blessed if we behold God's grandeur in this holy season. For if even cats, anticipate … how much more should we honor … Jesus Christ, the King?

"This will be a sign to you: You will find a baby wrapped in cloths and lying in a manger."
Luke 2:12 NIV

The Silhouette:
Under a star, the Light of the World was found, to be the illumination for all mankind. Will you allow the Christ-Child to be Your beacon? Will you behold Him as Messiah, Adonai, and as the One Who will one day return for His own? The Babe of the manger was the gift to all mankind. Is there room in your heart to receive Him?

Appendix

Muffin

It's said that God made kitty cats,
That we may touch a tiger.
Within those sparkling eyes I see,
A wild beast—yet one so tender.

Joyfully he chases,
A special toy or flower.
Anything that moves about,
He attacks with such power.

Some would say he's spoiled,
So much like a child,
One minute tormented,
The next lovable, even mild.

He likes to be fed promptly,
Or he "cries" with great protest,
Winding around the legs he sees,
Loving—giving his "caress."

If he wants to be cuddled,
He'll look for your lap,
Padding and purring sweetly,
His paws "tap, tap, tap."

This is a poem about our Muffin,
A part for you to see.
He is so very special,
To Douglas and to me.

Muffin's affection was his most precious quality. He loved to cuddle and "pad-and-purr." In fact, you could hear his rumbly love from several feet away. He slept in my arms at night and sought out my company throughout the day. He was a lap-cat and a helper with laundry and other chores.

God's love reaches down, around, and into—your every thought and activity. He is with His children at all times. His love is above, below and beside us. He is with us through the valleys and travels with us onward to the mountain tops. He's with us when we praise, when we cry out, and when we pause, questioning "why."

God's love is fathomless, fearless—He chases after us. It is relentless and abounding in grace and loving-kindness. Draw near and you just may hear the Lion of Judah "purr." For those who love Him, see and hear His voice—majestically and wondrously—in so many ways!

Leaving a Paw Print

Psalm 36:5-6, Deuteronomy 7:9, Romans 5:8, Romans 8:37-39,
1 John 3:1, 1 John 4:9-11, Jeremiah 31:3, Titus 3:4-5

Jeeper-Joy

"Jeeper-Joy,"
She's our "baby girl,"
Her charm, affection, and personality,
—Are the treasure of this "little pearl."

She's determined and playful,
With bright, shining eyes,
They sparkle with devilment!—as if saying,
"What trouble can I devise?"

If you tempt her—put before her,
A string, ribbon, or cord,
She'll begin playing,
The game—"tug-of-war."

This black and white "fur-ball,"
Has healthy, silky, fur;
She's as soft as velvet,
Can you hear her delicate purr?

She'll sing you a greeting,
With a melodic "chirp" or "meow,"
Then leave you wondering …
"Where can she be—now?"

Jeepers has added so much,
To our love-filled home.
This sweet little "minx,"
Will be with us—wherever we roam!!

Joy was perhaps the sweetest legacy of our second cat. She seemed to constantly fill our home with her lyrical songs. It's a good model to emulate. Unlike happiness, that tends to move and shift with our circumstances, joy—is a steadfast quality, decision or choice that we make—it's a state of of being. It means allowing God to create a safe place in our minds where He is our strength, our peace, our hope and refuge. Joy—cannot help but stand out in this world, when we are experiencing difficulty or hardship, for its presence will be written upon our faces and flow from within us like Jeeper's trills and meows.

Joy—keeps us praising God when others do not, because we are held securely by the One Who holds yesterday, today and tomorrow. That kind of faith causes joy to bubble up and burst out of a believer. Do you have a trill that gets noticed? How does knowing Jesus help you maintain a steady sense of His joy?

Our Tiger Lily

It's difficult to capture,
All of her qualities.
For this little fur-ball,
Has endless energy.
She has sparkly eyes full of mischief,
And is a flower-child.
She is friendly, and lovable,
Curious, playful, mild.
But sometimes she's ornery,
And is very easily, riled.
She is perfectly kissable,
And meets us at the door.
Who could love,
This "penny-pup," any more?
She knocks things off the counter,
Is a thief-of-hearts,
Then comes close,
While my works, I compose.
She is a peek-a-boo-baby,
Who loves to hide,
—Fetching me,
If I'm not, right by her side.
She lives up to the Tiger,
The first part of her name,
And is sweet like the Lily, implies.
She goes here and there,
All around the house,
Chasing the sun,
From the moment of its rise.
She reminds me,
To keep my eyes on You,
As my Master and my Friend.
Thank You, oh God,
For giving me,
This sweet,
Little feline friend.

As you can see from her description, Tilly has many facets to her personality. Each of us, does too. And God can use every nuance for His glory and service. Lord, it's our prayer that as we surrender our minds, hearts, and "paws" that You use us to fulfill Your plans and purposes. Help us to be a blessing to You and others, we pray. Amen.

Leaving a Paw Print

1 Samuel 16:7, Romans 12:4-6, 2 Peter 1:5-7, Genesis 1:26-27, Ephesians 2:10, Psalm 139:16, 1 Peter 4:10-11

Epilogue

I hope you've enjoyed our Christmas introduction to our new *Purry Companion's Series.* In it, we've traced the Biblical account of the birth of Jesus. We've explored how *even* felines seem to anticipate all the wonderful things that come alive and happen during the holiday season. And we've seen how God's love for all creatures, all creation and mankind, displays why He came to earth in the first place—to draw every heart to Himself—as a Master and Companion. God longs for us to share in His presence—peace, joy, and comfort—not just at Christmas, but everyday.

As we've done so, we've been meditating, spending time in companionship with Jesus. We've given you room to write your own prayers and time to explore what He wants to speak into your heart through Scripture. We've lifted our eyes, our paws in pause, our hearts to give God honor—all by magnifying one of His most intriguing creatures, the cat, in order to exalt Our Creator!

What's next? You'll have to check our Website to see where our *Creation's Kaleidoscope, Purry Companion's,* and God's Spirit and inspirations, take us.

Thanks for joining us. Until next time, we wish you blessed days in the sun, wonderful, growing relationship with Jesus, and purrs of praise unto your Master.

With warmest regards,
deborah goshorn-stenger

Also by *Deborah Goshorn-Stenger*

Available Now:

The *Purry Companion's* Series:
Happy, Meowy Christmas, Devotional

Creation's Kaleidoscope Series:
Embracing Light Devotional
Embracing Light Journal
*Embracing Light To-Go**

Check out our Website for the release dates of:

Creation's Kaleidoscope Series:
*Let Everything that Has Life ... Praise (Volume II)
Devotional, Journal, and To-Go Journal**
&
The Purry Companion's Series:
Paws to Ponder (Book I) Devotional

*Exclusively from our Website

To Contact us: 2PauseandPraiseCreations.com
or by mail at:
　　　　　2 Pause and Praise Creations
　　　　　5315 Long St, Suite 518
　　　　　McFarland, WI 53558

"The Lord bless you and keep you; the Lord make His face shine upon you, and be gracious to you; the Lord lift up His countenance upon you, and give you peace." Numbers 6:24-26 NKJV

Dear Readers,

Will you leave a kind or thoughtful review?

Now that you've finished reading this devotional, will you tell us what you think? Did God use *Happy, Meowy Christmas* to teach you that He is near, not just in this holy season, but everyday of the year? Did it encourage you to pause and behold the miracle of Jesus' birth? Did you offer the Lord a gift (of thankfulness, of yourself or service—an action) because He revealed His great love through His Word?

We'd be honored if you take time to leave us a comment (wherever you've purchased our product, i.e. Amazon, Apple, etc.). We'll use your feedback to guide any updates to this manuscript, as well as consider your inputs for future projects.

Would you like to be added to our mailing list?

You're invited to Join our E-Mailing List. Catch a Weekly Inspiration, "Peer Into" new products and learn a little more about us.

You can do so, at our website:

2pauseandpraisecreations.com

Thank you so much!
Doug, Deb & Tiger Lily

SHE'S A GOOD GIRL, CAN YOU HEAR HER GENTLE PURR?

He's a sweet cat, all curled up in a ball.

Cats steal our hearts, provide love, are independent, yet want to be near. They entertain us with their antics. THEY CAN HISS TO CONVEY THEIR "WISHES."

They can run and play, then be found catnapping moments later. They like to be fed promptly. THEY LOVE COMPLETELY, AND ARE A GREAT MODEL OF FORGIVENESS. *The feline is a gift from the Creator, to show us the many facets of His nature, wild and tame.* To hold a cat is to know, bliss. To adopt one, is to know sweet companionship. AS WE SPEND TIME WITH THEM, THEY SEEM TO INVEST IN US. *That's a lot like Jesus: He wants to be Your (and my) Best Friend.*

www.ingramcontent.com/pod-product-compliance
Lightning Source LLC
Chambersburg PA
CBHW050444150626
46551CB00028B/1417